THE BIG SECRET

Published by CelebrityPress®, Orlando, FL.

CelebrityPress® is a registered trademark.

Printed in the United States of America.

ISBN: 978-0-9983690-2-0
LCCN: 2016963456

This publication is designed to provide accurate and authoritative information with regard to the subject matter covered. It is sold with the understanding that the publisher is not engaged in rendering legal, accounting, or other professional advice. If legal advice or other expert assistance is required, the services of a competent professional should be sought. The opinions expressed by the authors in this book are not endorsed by CelebrityPress® and are the sole responsibility of the author rendering the opinion.

Most CelebrityPress® titles are available at special quantity discounts for bulk purchases for sales promotions, premiums, fundraising, and educational use. Special versions or book excerpts can also be created to fit specific needs.

For more information, please write:
CelebrityPress®
520 N. Orlando Ave, #2
Winter Park, FL 32789
or call 1.877.261.4930

Visit us online at: www.CelebrityPressPublishing.com

THE BIG SECRET

CelebrityPress®
Winter Park, Florida

CONTENTS

CHAPTER 1

MASTERING THE ART OF SUCCESS

BY JACK CANFIELD

It's often been said that success is a team sport. It's not just what you know, it's also *who* you know. And while you may be able to create tremendous success on your own, traveling the path of success with others makes the journey more enjoyable. Plus, the added accountability will propel you to success faster (and further) than you originally envisioned.

In my career, success in any undertaking has come down to not just *who I know*—but also *who I have on my team.* Along the way, I've learned a number of success principles that can now help you build your own network of influencers, mentors and experts—and develop a support team of people who can help you succeed.

BUILD YOUR PERSONAL NETWORK OF INFLUENCERS AND EXPERTS BY DEVELOPING GENUINE RELATIONSHIPS

One of the most important skills for success in today's world, especially for entrepreneurs and business owners, is networking. Jim Bunch, the creator of the Ultimate Game of Life, once stated, "Your network will determine your net worth." In my life this has proven to be true. The more time I have spent consciously building and nurturing my network of advisers, colleagues, clients, students and fans, the more successful I have become.

Businesses and careers are built on relationships, and relationships form when people meet and interact with each other over time in an authentic and caring way. As I'm sure you're aware, statistics confirm over and over that people prefer to do business with people they know, respect and trust.

Effective networking, therefore, is all about developing relationships.

Your goal for networking

In developing your own personal network, your job is to seek out people who know what you don't—and who can help you connect where you can't. Initially, your goal shouldn't be to make a sale, but instead to seek advice, connections, recommendations and insights. To the extent that you can provide something in return, do so. But remember that developing genuine relationships that you can call upon at any time—for years into the future, potentially—takes time and consideration. It requires careful thought and a mindfulness for others.

My good friend Ivan Misner, founder of the international networking phenomenon BNI Worldwide, explains that good networking is a combination of three things: visibility, credibility and profitability.

Visibility is you and another individual becoming aware of each other. The individual—who may be a source of information, referrals to people who can help you or even a potential customer—may learn about you through your public relations, social media or advertising efforts—or through someone you both know. Soon, you might become personally acquainted and communicate on a first-name basis. That's visibility.

Credibility means you take the next step and become reliable and worthy of the other person's confidence. You begin to form expectations of each other and those expectations are fulfilled. Credibility increases when appointments are kept, promises are acted upon, facts are verified, and services are rendered. The old saying, Results speak louder than words, is true. Credibility also comes from third parties. Will someone they know vouch for you? Are you honest? Is your project or business legitimate? Are you effective? Are you someone who can be counted on in a crunch? If you are, your credibility will grow—as will important and beneficial relationships.

Profitability is what comes from mature relationships (business or personal) that are mutually rewarding and where both people gain something from the connection. This stage may be reached quickly—such as when an urgent need arises—or it may take years. Most likely, it's somewhere in between. Of course, much depends on the quality of your interaction with each other—but most especially on the desire of both parties to move the relationship forward.

My closest and most productive network

Of course, profiting from relationships isn't limited to making money from a new customer or getting a referral. It may come in the form of a connection to someone who can help you launch a new initiative or otherwise grow your business. It may include access to a mentor or a professional adviser or a contact in another industry who can help you expand your market. It might be the ability to delegate more of your workload, gain substantial free time for your hobby or personal interests—or spend more quality time with your family.

My closest and most productive network has included my business partner Patty Aubery and my *Success Principles* coauthor Janet Switzer—two women who've not only been close friends and colleagues for 25 years, but who have also developed a robust and influential network *from which I've benefitted.* <u>By combining their own contact lists with people I know, we've generated millions of dollars in business, accumulated 1 million Facebook fans, and produced millions of customers, clients and students who follow *The Success Principles.*</u> Our combined contact lists are filled with hundreds of key individuals who can help out with advice, direction, a name, an idea, resources, marketing assistance and more. At any time, we can ask each other, W*ho do we know who can help with this new initiative?* . . . confident that we can get our needs and wants addressed within days. That's the real "profitability" of a network.

FORM A MASTERMIND GROUP TO KEEP YOU FOCUSED, ENTHUSIASTIC AND INNOVATIVE

One of the most powerful tools for success ever identified is a process called *masterminding.* We all know that two heads are better than one when it comes to solving a problem or creating a result. So imagine having a permanent group of five to six people who meet regularly for the purpose of problem-solving, brainstorming, networking, encouraging and motivating each other.

Napoleon Hill first wrote about mastermind groups in 1937 in his classic book *Think and Grow Rich*. All the world's richest industrialists— from the early 20th Century to today's modern icons of business— have harnessed the power of the mastermind group. In fact, it's the one concept achievers reference most when they credit any one thing with helping them become successful.

Millions have discovered that a mastermind group can focus special energy on your efforts—in the form of knowledge, new ideas, introductions, a vast array of resources, and, most important, spiritual energy. It's this spiritual aspect that Napoleon Hill wrote about extensively. He said that if we are in tune with the mastermind—that is, God, Source, the universal power, Infinite Intelligence—we have significantly more positive energy available to us, a power that can be focused on our success.

How a mastermind group works

A mastermind group is made up of people who come together on a regular basis—weekly, biweekly, or monthly—to share ideas, thoughts, information, feedback, contacts, and resources. By getting the perspective, knowledge, experience, and resources of others in the group, not only can you greatly expand your own limited view of the world, you can also advance your own goals and projects more quickly.

A mastermind group can be composed of people from your own industry or profession—or people from different walks of life. It can focus on business issues, personal issues or both. But for a mastermind group to be powerfully effective, people must be comfortable enough with each other to tell the truth. Some of the most valuable feedback I have ever received has come from members of my mastermind group confronting me about overcommitting, selling my services too cheaply, focusing on the trivial, not delegating enough, thinking too small, and playing it safe.

If you're not in a mastermind group already, I recommend that you form one (or join one) as soon as possible.

Mastermind groups nurture new ideas and initiatives

In 2010, Jill Douka of Athens, Greece left my *Breakthrough to Success* training with the commitment to be part of a mastermind group with five other attendees from different countries. When the economic downturn in Greece began affecting her local network, Jill looked forward to meeting with her global mastermind group on Skype and Google Hangouts—spending an hour every other week using words other than default, unemployment and debt.

Before long, Jill learned through her mastermind group about TED talks and gave her first international speech in Chennai, India. On the plane trip home, an idea took shape in her mind: what if instead of just one TED talk, Jill created positive-focused, interactive events—then made videos of them available on YouTube so people around the world could benefit?

While civil unrest and economic problems in Greece made Jill hesitant to discuss her idea with colleagues in Athens, her mastermind group was enthusiastic. With their constant encouragement and support, Jill held the first one-day workshop in Athens to a jam-packed audience of 500 attendees and 300 livestream participants—all supported by 70 volunteers and 57 corporate sponsors. The feedback was tremendous. The following November, Sergio Sedas—another of my graduates—produced the second such event in Mexico—with more than 4,000 people participating in interactive solution-focused workshops given by presenters from the United States, Mexico, Canada, and Bermuda.

What could a mastermind group do for you?

FIND A MENTOR AND FOLLOW THEIR ADVICE

Another key strategy that successful people use is to constantly seek out experts in their field for advice, direction and information. The truth is there are countless people who've triumphed over the specific hardship you're facing—or who have succeeded in your specific area of endeavor. Why not take advantage of all that wisdom and experience by finding a mentor who has already been down the road you want to travel?

All you have to do is ask.

It's easier than you think

While it may seem daunting at first to contact successful people and ask for ongoing advice and assistance, it's easier than you think to enlist the mentorship of those who are far ahead of you in the areas in which you'd like to succeed.

What mentors do more than anything, says famed speaker and bestselling author Les Brown, is help you see possibilities. In other words, mentors help you overcome "possibility blindness" both by acting as a role model for you and by conveying a certain level of expectation as they communicate with you.

When Les started his speaking career in the early 1980s, he sent a cassette tape of his earliest keynote speech to the late Dr. Norman Vincent Peale, the world-renowned speaker and publisher of Guideposts magazine. That cassette tape led to a long and fruitful relationship for Les, as Dr. Peale not only took Les under his wing and counseled him on his speaking style, but also quietly opened doors and helped Les get important speaking engagements.

Perhaps like Les, you just need someone to open doors for you. Or perhaps you need a referral to a technical expert who can help you build a new service for your company. Maybe you simply need validation that the path you're pursuing is the right one. A mentor can help you with all of these things, but you need to be prepared to ask for specific advice.

Do your homework

One of the easiest ways to research the names and backgrounds of people who have been successful in your field is to read industry magazines, search the Internet, ask trade association executive directors, attend trade shows and conventions, call fellow entrepreneurs, or approach others who operate in your industry or profession.

Look for mentors who have the kind of well-rounded experience you need to tackle your goal. When you start seeing a pattern of the same few people being recommended, you know you've identified your short list of possible mentors.

The Success Principles coauthor Janet Switzer regularly mentors people on how to grow their small business. When Lisa Miller of CRA Management Group called Janet, she was just about to sign away a large percentage of her revenues to someone she thought would help her develop a new area of her business. Janet showed Lisa how to instantly accomplish the same goal without outside parties and even helped her land new business from existing clients, accelerating Lisa's company growth plan by four months and earning her hundreds of thousands of extra dollars.

To contact possible mentors like Janet and ensure a successful conversation once you do, make a list of specific points you'd like to cover in your first conversation, such as why you'd like them to mentor you and what kind of help you might be looking for. Be brief, but be confident, too.

The truth is that successful people like to share what they have learned with others. It's a human trait to want to pass on wisdom. Not everyone will take the time to mentor you, but many will if asked. You simply need to make a list of the people you would like to have as your mentor and ask them to devote a few minutes a month to you.

Some will say no, but some will say yes. Keep asking people until you get a positive response.

Follow their advice and return the favor

Mentors don't like to have their time wasted. So when you seek out their advice, follow it. Study their methods, ask your questions, make sure you understand the process—then, as much as is humanly possible, follow your mentor's suggestions. Try them on and see how they work for you. You can always adjust and improve upon them as you go along.

Be prepared to give your mentors something in return, too—even if it's something simple such as keeping them updated on industry information or calling with new opportunities that might benefit them. Look for ways to give back to your mentors. Help others, too. What a great reward to any mentor—to eventually have their former protégé out in the world mentoring others!

BUILD A POWERFUL TEAM THAT LETS YOU FOCUS ON YOUR CORE GENIUS

Every high achiever has a powerful team of key staff members, consultants, vendors, and helpers who do the bulk of the work while he or she is free to create new sources of income and new opportunities for success. The world's greatest philanthropists, athletes, entertainers, professionals, and others also have people who manage projects and handle everyday tasks—enabling them to do more for others, hone their craft, practice their sport and so on.

To help you clarify what you should be spending your time on and what you should be delegating to others, I recommend an exercise called *The Total Focus Process.* The goal is to find the top one, two or three activities that best use your core genius, bring you the most money, and produce the greatest level of enjoyment.

1. *Start by listing those activities that occupy your time,* whether they're business-related, personal or volunteer work. List even small tasks like returning phone calls, filing or photocopying.
2. *Choose from this list those one, two or three things* you're particularly brilliant at, your special talents—those unique things very few other people can do as well as you. Also choose from this list the three activities that generate the most income for you or your company. Any activities that you are brilliant at and that generate the most income for you or your company are activities you'll want to focus on.
3. *Finally, create a plan for delegating remaining activities to others.* Delegating takes time and training, but over time you can off-load the nonessential tasks on your list until you are doing less of the ones with little payoff—and more of what you're really good at. That is how you create a brilliant career.

Seek out key "staff" members and advisors

If you're a business owner or career professional, start training key people to take over the tasks you identified above. If you're a one-person business, start looking for a dynamic number-two person who could handle your projects, book your sales transactions, and completely take over other tasks while you concentrate on what you do best. If philanthropic pursuits or community projects are your "business," there are volunteers you can "hire" to help you—including college interns, who may work solely for class credit.

And if you are a stay-at-home parent, your most valuable "staff" will be your house cleaner, your babysitter and other people who can help you get away for time by yourself or with your spouse. A part-time helper can do grocery shopping, get your car washed, pick up the kids or pick up the dry cleaning—all for a modest wage. If you're a single parent, these folks are even more important to your successful future.

In addition to business and personal helpers, high achievers typically have a powerful team of *professional* advisors to turn to for support. Today's world is a complicated place. Professional advisors—such as your banker, your lawyers, a high-net-worth certified public accountant, your investment counselor, your doctor, nutritionist, personal trainer, and the leader of your religious organization—can walk you through challenges and opportunities, saving you time, effort and usually money. If you run a business, these advisors are essential.

BUILD A COMMUNITY AND PASS ON YOUR LEGACY

To truly master the art of success, you also need to pursue one more critical activity: building a community of followers who can join you in expanding your work, fulfilling your vision and—most importantly—securing your legacy.

Virtually all great thinkers of our age have managed to pass down their wisdom and life's work once they can no longer be active. Today, that "act of succession" is easier than ever.

The Internet and social media makes it possible

Today, social media has hit the tipping point where we're now seeing millions of followers convert into fellow devotees, passionate advocates, enthusiastic buyers, and committed partners for social change. Building a community of followers for your work or philanthropic pursuit guarantees there will be a network of people to join you in virtually any venture you want to pursue.

The key is to attract followers who will stay engaged with you and your message—then pass on your information to their own friends, colleagues and fans. To reach that goal, you'll want to maintain an ongoing presence on the most popular social media sites including Facebook, LinkedIn and Twitter.

While you can spend time writing your own posts and articles, then master the technology needed to "boost" your social media activity, I recommend you check out: Social5Marketing.com/details, a done-for-you service that provides a team of world-class writers from top publications with smart online marketers to write, post and even run advertising for you on the major social-media platforms.

Best of all, your online activity is scheduled, managed, executed and tracked for less than you'd pay your teenager. Whether you use this service (which also writes your blog, does email marketing and helps generate prospective buyers for your business or cause), you'll want to establish a personal brand, build your online presence, and pursue community building as an activity to ultimately support your success.

About Jack

Known as America's #1 Success Coach, Jack Canfield is the CEO of the Canfield Training Group in Santa Barbara, CA, which trains and coaches entrepreneurs, corporate leaders, managers, sales professionals and the general public in how to accelerate the achievement of their personal, professional and financial goals.

Jack Canfield is best known as the coauthor of the #1 New York Times bestselling *Chicken Soup for the Soul®* book series, which has sold more than 500 million books in 47 languages, including 11 New York Times #1 bestsellers. As the CEO of Chicken Soup for the Soul Enterprises he helped grow the *Chicken Soup for the Soul®* brand into a virtual empire of books, children's books, audios, videos, CDs, classroom materials, a syndicated column and a television show, as well as a vigorous program of licensed products that includes everything from clothing and board games to nutraceuticals and a successful line of *Chicken Soup for the Pet Lover's Soul®* cat and dog foods.

His other books include *The Success Principles*™: *How to Get from Where You Are to Where You Want to Be* (recently revised as the 10th Anniversary Edition), *The Success Principles for Teens, The Aladdin Factor, Dare to Win, Heart at Work, The Power of Focus: How to Hit Your Personal, Financial and Business Goals with Absolute Certainty, You've Got to Read This Book, Tapping into Ultimate Success, Jack Canfield's Key to Living the Law Attraction,* and his recent novel—*The Golden Motorcycle Gang: A Story of Transformation.*

Jack is a dynamic speaker and was recently inducted into the National Speakers Association's Speakers Hall of Fame. He has appeared on more than 1000 radio and television shows including Oprah, Montel, Larry King Live, the Today Show, Fox and Friends, and 2 hour-long PBS Specials devoted exclusively to his work. Jack is also a featured teacher in 12 movies including *The Secret, The Meta-Secret, The Truth, The Keeper of the Keys, Tapping into the Source,* and *The Tapping Solution.*

Jack has personally helped hundreds of thousands of people on six different continents become multi-millionaires, business leaders, best-selling authors, leading sales professionals, successful entrepreneurs, and world-class athletes while at the same time creating balanced, fulfilling and healthy lives.

His corporate clients have included Virgin Records, SONY Pictures, Daimler-Chrysler, Federal Express, GE, Johnson & Johnson, Merrill Lynch, Campbell's Soup, Re/Max, The Million Dollar Forum, The Million Dollar Roundtable, The Entrepreneur Organization, The Young Presidents Organization, the Executive Committee, and the World Business Council.

He is the founder of the Transformational Leadership Council and a member of Evolutionary Leaders, two groups devoted to helping create a world that works for everyone.

Jack is a graduate of Harvard, earned his M.Ed. from the University of Massachusetts and has received three honorary doctorates in psychology and public service. He is married, has three children, two step-children and a grandson.

For more information, visit:
- www.JackCanfield.com

CHAPTER 2

FOCUSING ON SUCCESS IN REAL ESTATE

IT'S SIMPLER THAN YOU MAY HAVE IMAGINED

BY KIMBERLY DENNEY

Your system for success should never spread yourself thin.

I've worked in the real estate industry a long time. I started out as an agent and then became a national trainer for some of the world's most elite real estate companies. During these sessions, I'd help serious and committed agents learn how to master their craft and maximize their results. It was fun, and of course, it was rewarding. But through all of these efforts to inspire others to reach their full potential, I found myself missing the action that came with the game of real estate. I missed being an agent, and it spurred on a challenge to my own self! Could I re-enter the industry and achieve more than I had before I left it, and as much as I'd helped others achieve through my work in the classroom? Well, a Texas girl is always up for a good challenge so…challenge accepted!

When I got back into the swing of things and saw all the other agents around me in action, I learned something big. And this, I assure you, is THE BIG SECRET—too many agents spread themselves far too thin.

That sounds simplistic, but there are many reasons why spreading yourself too thin can lead to your own downfall, or the burn-out that leads to you no longer loving what you do. That's a pretty lousy place to be, regardless of what your chosen career is. If you could avoid it, would you? If you could find a system that helped deter against that, you'd be happy, right? Well, I'll be honest, my hope is to find a team of people to train with under me that will embrace this system and use it the way it's been proven most effective. I'm not perfect and I'll always have areas of improvement, but I know that I have one reoccurring factor that other Realtors® would find enviable:

I've found that my contacts and connections help me to sell properties quickly—sometimes before I even put them onto the MLS.

It's exciting to be able to share with you the simple strategies that lead to super success. Revealing this secret can help you 'up your game' whether you are already active in or interested in entering into real estate. It's about more than handing over those keys; it's about giving people the keys that will drive their success. Being a mentor in that process is the reward of my efforts; the way I can give back to my community, which has given me so much.

THREE THINGS A REALTOR® CAN DO TO STAND APART

A little extra effort upfront can lead to you becoming the type of expert that helps potential clients garner instant confidence in your abilities.

I'm not saying that I am the only person to ever have done these things I'm suggesting, but I can guarantee you that I am one of a small handful— small enough that I am yet to meet another person in my career who has done them.

1. **If becoming an expert is your goal, working too hard isn't the answer; working smart is.**
   In those nighttime hours, it isn't always enjoyable to go that extra mile to listen to a city or county council meeting, but it is very important if anything on their agenda is related to roads, buildings, real estate, property taxes, schools, or development. Through my faithful attendance to these meetings (when there is a topic that impacts my business) is being discussed, I often know what to expect

well before sellers and other people who work in real estate related careers. This gives me the opportunity to offer valuable insight that is beneficial to potential sellers and purchasers of property. Due diligence is a part of our Code of Ethics that has been established by the National Association of Realtors®. It does matter.

2. Gain access to as much real estate information as you can for your market.

In my community of Anna, Texas, we are a growing and thriving community. There is much new construction and many professionals moving into the area constantly, as well as moving out. Knowing this only gives me an edge if I know what to do with that information. What I've chosen to do is collect as many of the house plans and specs from as many builders as possible in my area. Because of this, I can go to a listing appointment or approach a potential seller with a plethora of information about their property that is quite specific. I earn their trust and business with knowledge and proven results, not just with a sales pitch that I'll give them my best. I've already shown that, and what a difference that does make. What things can you do to make sure you know as much information as possible about the community you live in? Chances are you won't find a bottleneck of competition at that place. My personal motto is: There's never a traffic jam in the extra mile. It's yet to prove me wrong!

3. Find your market and stick with it.

This is where most agents currently fall short. You cannot become an expert by attempting to be all things to people everywhere. Before I went into training, I'd take listings everywhere, but I don't do that anymore. Listings for people outside of my town makes no sense when it comes to time, efficiency, and offering the best service I can. As a result, I can get to a house I have listed within ten minutes to show a property if I get a call. My clients are prepared for this and together, we make sure we can take advantage of hot leads when they come our way. Occasionally, this even involves the pets and getting them out of a home so we can show it. When there's a will, there's a way!

It'll never be as easy as 1, 2, 3, but using the 1, 2, 3, I shared will do wonders to help you establish your reputation as a Realtor® who is involved in their community and their business. There's a saying in Texas that applies to this type of commitment and what it offers:

Shine like a Lone Star pearl.

And shine, you shall. The thought of mentoring individuals that cultivate into pearls motivates me.

BUILDING LASTING CONNECTIONS, NOT COSTLY CONNECTIONS

How we market ourselves will always be a buzz phrase for anyone who works in a commission-based industry. How much money do you spend and where? How do you monitor your results so you know what's effective?

This is another area where agents often get overwhelmed, because they make things complicated when they don't have to be. At times, even when it challenges our perceptions, simplicity offers the best results. We can build great connections for our business without spending a fortune or thinking we have to be overly elaborate.

What I love about these ideas are that they can adapt to everyone, using what you have available to you and allowing your personality to shine. Knowledge is necessary, but personality is too! They go hand in hand when you're creating a business as a self-employed individual.

1. **Enjoy a nice, cold drink—from me to you.**
   Friday and Saturday are garage sale days in Texas, and that means there is an opportunity to get to meet a bunch of great, friendly folks at one time. I always have a cooler packed with water in my vehicle so I can stop at these events, or if I see someone working hard on their yard, or even city workers. People remember this and with a little friendly conversation, you'd be amazed at how quickly you can get referrals on the spot. If I get one referral for every one hundred bottles of water that I hand out, it's safe to say that the water has more than paid off.

   When it comes to print ad funds, they are typically a waste of valuable resources for one simple reason: how can you stand out on a piece of black and white paper, amongst a sea of other agents on that same paper? You can't! So, why waste funds with that? You could buy enough water to actually go and meet many people face to face.

2. Make your vehicle known.

My vehicle is easy to identify—a purple Mini Cooper convertible with me behind the wheel. And in the trunk? That is where you will find a matching cooler for those bottles of water that are always with me. Some people do fancy car wraps and you certainly can if it's within your budget; however, don't feel like you have to go that big. In what way can you make your car be remembered by everyone you pass by?

3. Take care of the little details for your clients without any hassles.

I own and run a successful management company, which keeps me busy in addition to all of the real estate work that I do. In order to do this, having a handyman that I can rely on is essential. It's almost inevitable that someone is going to move into a home and notice some little problem or another, and when that happens, they know they can call me and my guy will be over there to take care of business. They appreciate the thought, and when they know that I am committed to them after their transaction is complete they know that they've found a Realtor® for life.

4. Be consistent with your efforts.

Whether you do a newsletter, telephone call, or an event, make sure you do it consistently. The last thing you want to say that you're going to do is follow-up quarterly with clients (hoping to earn some coveted referrals) and then you do not. Rest assured, they'll forget about you. The way that I do this is through fun—for both me and my past real estate clients and rental property tenants. I host events where we can keep our connections strong and really built a sense of unity. I look forward to these so much and everyone else seems to, as well—they come, so at least I believe they do. We have food, beverages, maybe music, and camaraderie.

What things can you think of that would be different, affordable, and effective for your business? Ideas are endless and when you generate an idea that resonates with who you are as a person and your specific goals in real estate, you're going to find that you are no longer a secret in your community. People know you and people want your services.

PARTICIPATING IN OUR SUCCESS IS MANDATORY IN LIFE

When you find a career that you love and your hard work starts to pay off, you know that it's a privilege and opportunity to find a way to spread the word.

Every day has gone by in a whir since I decided to return to practicing real estate after being a trainer. My days are busy and long, but the rewards and joys in the moments I play witness to every day continue to inspire me and motivate me. To get here it took:

1. Research to determine my market.
2. Knowledge of my market.
3. Serving my market.

The fact that I can now say that I've "been there, done that" is wonderful. Knowing that I have a way to help others gain that same expertise and experience is rewarding. Peoples' lives are made better by these types of successes. I have learned that you cannot avoid success when you serve others, and without a doubt, it's one of the best lessons I have learned in my life.

About Kimberly

Kimberly Denney started out as an agent who became a national trainer for some of the world's most elite real estate companies. She helps committed agents to learn how to master their craft and maximize their results. As time passed, she also built a business with strict guidelines by using a three-leveled plan: research to determine her market, knowledge of her market, and serving her market. She realized that her hometown Anna, Texas was a high-growth area that she felt was the market for her.

"There's never a traffic jam in the extra mile."

CHAPTER 3

SO WHAT'S THE *BIG* SECRET?

BY VKARA PHIFER-SMITH

> *The greatest secrets are always hidden*
> *in the most unlikely places.*
> **~ Roald Dahl**

All the ancients, mystics, shaman, alchemists, Free Masons, Rosicrucians and other esoteric groups and secret societies knew that …

THE BIG SECRET IS YOU!

You have been present through all the good, bad and ugly in your life. If something is 'wrong' and needs to change in your life – guess what? That 'something' is You! If all is right and wonderful in your world, guess why? It's because of *You*!

You were the one who decided to heed your inner voice to begin your healing from a bitter disappointment or the devastating loss of a loved one. *You* decided when enough was enough and that you had cried your last tear.

When you are applauded for an achievement and you, gratefully, thank those who were there for you, remember to save the biggest 'Thank You' for yourself. *You* are the one who did the work for this accomplishment, so 'own' it.

You are at the forefront of your most successful accomplishments and at ground zero of your deepest regret. *You* have made the decisions that caused your own destruction or glory.

Remarkable research in neuroscience and epigenetics is providing proof to long-held fantastic theories about the true nature of our reality and expanding our collective knowledge exponentially.

Thanks to many brilliant research organizations, scientists and new-thought agents like the Heart Math Institute, Jack Canfield, Deepak Chopra, Dr. Joe Dispenza, Dr. Bruce Lipton, Marianne Williamson, Michael Beckwith and Gregg Braden to name a few, we are now on the brink of a game-changing merger of science and spirit.

The new information by way of numerous articles, books and blogs that *You* are at the very instant, the Point Zero of when, where, how and why anything and everything materializes into physical reality and thus your life is spreading like a wild fire in our collective mind.

The Big Secret that *You* are both 'The Observer' and 'The Architect' of your life is no longer a secret. *You* are that powerful. Each of us has that power and together we co-create our world – our collective reality. Therefore, *You* have a unique opportunity to consciously take ownership of your life - to fearlessly create changes in your world in the most intriguing and transformative ways.

I recall the one experience in my life that changed everything for me – flipped my script, shifted my being and took me forever beyond victimization and helplessness to absolute ownership of my life. This experience sparked the wild fire of understanding that I was, beyond any doubt, orchestrating the events in my life and creating my reality.

This was the seminal experience where I knew that...*I Am The Big Secret!*

The Erte Experience

It was Erte, the legendary Art Deco artist! I might be sick. I gasped and held my breath, willing myself out of the throws of nausea, as I heard feet shuffling toward the door of the apartment on the Boulogne-sur-Seine. I stood looking down at my feet standing unsteadily on the doormat emboldened with the infamous initials, E.T. I drifted into a space somewhere outside of time. It felt eerily familiar, an intense déjà vu moment. All at once things came together in my mind – like seeing the inner workings of an intricate Brobdingnagian clock.

I was standing in a moment that I had dreamt of in great detail and repeatedly visualized. I had imagined being here at his door hearing the shuffle of his feet as he came to let me in, a thousand times.

"Aloe. Who is it please?" came the soft very French whisper.
"Vkara", I spoke up, snapping back to reality.
"Oh yes, Miss Vkara. Please do come in."

He smiled warmly extending a frail hand that matched his petit frame. Chills pervaded my being. I respectfully stepped inside and reverently scanned the exquisite apartment. Everything was exactly as it was when it was photographed for his autobiography some 30 years before. The glass case housing several generations of energetic white doves loomed lugubriously above us while he politely ushered me around his sacred space.

Erte had practically been a recluse for decades yet here he was, très beau in a dark olive three-piece suit accented by a vintage filigreed pocket watch and chain. I was a young single mom from a working-class environment doing my best to appear chic and refined on my first trip to Paris or anywhere outside the USA for that matter. I experienced each second with such awe and wonder. Every moment was confirmation that what I was now experiencing was the direct result of what I had imagined.

Erte poured Campari into two tall fancy glasses as we settled into the comfy chairs in the office where he had created his most famous designs and illustrations for Vogue and Harper's Bazaar. We talked for hours as if we had known each other for lifetimes. My heart skipped when he abruptly walked over to me, felt tip pen in hand, inviting me to sign the famous panel that he asked all his most special visitors to sign. The smooth wood panel had been signed by the likes of Grace Kelly, Wallace Simpson - now I was being given the honor. What were the odds that our first meeting would evolve into an unlikely friendship complete with spirited creative discussions and marvelous times in Paris, Barbados and New York?

I experienced, in real time, everything that I had imagined exactly the way that I visualized it. I imbued my dream with unprecedented emotional intensity and made epic moves that propelled me far beyond my comfort zone. I summoned resources I never knew I possessed to realize this dream. One of the most amazing things I found was that my 'Erte Experience' expanded upon itself and assumed a life of its own, continuing to delight and amaze me with stunning events and plot twists beyond my original expectations!

At this point in my life I had been solely focused on my growing fashion career, yet I was undergoing a profound shift. I discovered that I could help others to create extraordinary experiences of their own by sharing what I learned from my Erte Experience. For the next few years I continued to create fashion while also devoting myself to the rigorous work of self-realization and my own evolution.

I diligently applied the components of how I created my Erte Experience and combined them with what I was learning and discovering in all areas of my life. I created a radio show and developed workshops where I shared my knowledge with a growing following. My "Create Your Life" workshops morphed into a successful coaching business which has since undergone many evolutions to remain at the forefront of our ever-shifting times. Consequently, I have found a few components that are integral in creating extraordinary life experiences and the incredible reality you desire.

SEVEN COMPONENTS FOR CREATING YOUR EXTRAORDINARY LIFE

Imagination is everything. It is the preview
of life's coming attractions.
~ Einstein.

1. *IMAGINATION* is our ability to create something in our minds that doesn't yet exist. Imagination is responsible for many world-changing ideas. Steve Jobs imagined innovative products that changed the technology game forever. Elon Musk imagines living on Mars and 'gigafactories' that will power the Earth.

All of the biggest accomplishments in human history started as a thought fueled by imagination.

- *Imagine something* you wish to have or wish to achieve. Take a deep breath and visualize it in your mind's eye.
- *Set Your Intention* by being clear about what you want and why you want it.
- *Declare Your Intention* clearly and decisively by creating an affirmation or a mantra.

Dr. Martin Luther King imagined and penned a seemingly impossible story of freedom and declared it in his "I Have a Dream" speech. He painted a vivid picture of a future filled with equality, peace and love. It was so masterfully written and emotionally charged that people all over the planet were transfixed and instantly committed to being co-authors in his far-reaching dream. Delivering this speech like a virtuoso of vision and pronouncement, Dr. King reached into the well of human emotions as he took us to the depths of our common despair and then lifted us up with the shared hope for a brighter future. By the time his speech ended, we had ascended to the mountaintop with him and a multi-cultured generation made "I have a dream!" their collective mantra.

My visualizations and daydreams of meeting Erte were so vivid and felt so real that I decided to write them down. I put those separate images together into a story. By doing this, a desire to meet someone I admired expanded into a fantastic story that I believed would actually unfold in my life. I devoted quality time to writing my story for The Erte Experience. It overflowed with thrilling visuals and intense uplifting emotional triggers. I read it and visualized it until it was more real than what was actually occurring in my 'real' life.

> ***You can make anything by writing.***
> **~ C.S. Lewis**

2. *WRITE YOUR STORY* the way you imagine it unfolding. Writing and reading a story has profound meditative effects on the body. The effects on the brain are equally stunning. It stimulates multiple complex cognitive functions and increases blood flow to different areas of the brain. The very structure of a story – beginning, middle and end – helps the brain develop more plasticity, helping us think in sequence, more easily linking cause and effect.

Create an exciting beginning, a substantive middle where you get what you want and a positive successful 'continuation'. Instead of an ending, leave your story open ended. This allows the energy of your story to build upon itself creating space for surprising events beyond your wildest dreams to occur. Be very specific and give descriptive details. Include strong sensory elements that stimulate your imagination. Using rich visual, sensual and emotional texture will imbue your story with an undeniable realism.

3. EMPLOY YOUR SENSES

- *Sight* – Each color has its own particular wavelength and energy; therefore, it creates different moods. Make wise color choices depending on the mood you want to create for yourself.

- *Smell* – Smell is a powerful emotional trigger. Choose fragrances that evoke pleasant memories. Make reference to your favorite scents.

- *Hearing* – Choose sounds that evoke positive feelings and create desired moods, like your favorite music, church bells or birds singing. Create conversations you envision having.

- *Touch* – Incorporating textural descriptions like 'silky sheets' creates one physical sensation while a 'scratchy woolen sweater' evokes the opposite physical reaction in your body.

- *Taste* – The very thought of a juicy burger or a fresh green salad makes the mouth water and physically mobilizes the gastric juices. Including the experience of eating adds physical and emotional satisfaction.

Remember your story _must_ be full of all the sensory elements that stimulate, satisfy and evoke positive emotional responses in you. Be creative. You are imagining. Make it Awesome . . . Over the Top . . . Larger Than Life *and* GO FOR IT!

4. *VISUALIZE YOUR STORY* obsessively. Let it play over in your mind at every available moment. Experimenting with different forms of meditation and breathing techniques until you find the ones that work best for you will add an important dimension to your visualization experience.

5. *ACTIVATE YOUR PASSION* by allowing the intense desire you feel for what you want to resonate in your soul. Put the fulfillment of your story at the forefront of your life. Become obsessed with making it happen. A consistent regimen of movement such as aerobic exercise, walking, hiking, dancing practiced in tandem with a discipline like Tai Chi, Qigong or Yoga will intensify your energy levels and give you the ability to focus your energy toward the fulfillment of your story.

6. *PRACTICE GRATITUDE* consistently for just five minutes a day to lower levels of depression and stress and increase feelings of joy. Keep a gratitude journal. Take one minute each day to write down the people and things for which you are grateful. Send notes and cards of appreciation to family, friends and co-workers – just because. Don't forget to be grateful for who You are right now. Say THANK YOU out loud to yourself in different languages - Gracias, Vinaka, Merci, Asante, Danke, Mahalo.

> *We must find time to stop and thank the people who*
> *make a difference in our lives.*
> **~ John F. Kennedy**

I am grateful to my parents, Lawrence and Vernessia and my brother Antonio, who are now my angels. My brother, Lawrence, "J.R", who graciously provided a haven for me to heal and create. My brother, Tchai, for his warm jovial nature. My cousin, Lepena, for her grace, beauty and light. My lovely aunts, Barbara, Jean, Dot and Janice for their wise female energy. My friends Barbara and Rose, for many outrageous adventures! Steph, "Mr. L", for being 'solid' and 'real'. Dr. James Porterfield, the best cardiologist, ever. My family, friends, clients, challengers and champions for being a part of my evolution. My son-in-law Gary, who really 'gets me'. . . Most of all, to my awesome daughter Shinique, whose brilliant mind, creativity, love and support, I would literally not be here without.

7. *CELEBRATE YOURSELF* and what you accomplish at every phase as your story unfolds. No matter how small the achievement make a big deal over it and shortly it will expand in grander ways than you originally imagined. Plan an event and invite family and friends to join in your celebration. Lastly move through your world as if you know that. . .

The Big Secret is YOU!

About Vkara

Vkara Phifer-Smith is Founder and CEO of Mystic TREK. She is a successful coach to executives from Fortune 500 corporations such as Exxon, Merck, ATT, Lucent Technologies and Quintiles, as well as politicians and entrepreneurs. She is widely respected in the industry by her peers for her unique coaching style and her ability to impact profound transformation in the work place.

Vkara is the former talk radio host of *The Mind's Eye*, where she introduced her audience to the concepts of co-creation, stress management, meditation and many controversial topics decades before they became mainstream.

Vkara has studied vision and meditation techniques with respected masters from many global cultures, ultimately achieving esteemed positions in the upper echelons of their wisdom institutions. For over thirty years, Vkara has harmoniously blended cutting-edge discoveries in epigenetics, quantum physics and mind-body sciences with innovative thinking, mindfulness practices and creative expression.

Vkara and her team are currently hosting curated transformational treks for individuals and groups in exotic environments offering a combination of technologies: coaching, team building, intuitive perception, self-awareness, cultural immersion, physical challenges and fun.

Vkara's Favorite Quote:

The mind, once stretched by a new idea, never returns to its original dimensions.
~ Ralph Waldo Emerson

We all come from magic and Vkara has an elegant way of bringing out the magic in us.
~ Ruby Dee – Actress, Activist, Playwright, Poet

Vkara is a rare talent. I have worked with many success coaches as a client, colleague and even as a trainer, and I can say without a doubt that Vkara has an unusual gift. Her insights are clear and consistently accurate, her guidance is exact and pragmatic, and her style is simple, direct and always a pleasure. I do believe that any client of hers will not only feel satisfied, but fortunate.
~ Jonathan Ellerby, PhD – Best-selling author of
Return To The Sacred and *Inspiration Deficit Disorder*

Like most men, I sought answers to life's challenges from a logical, rational viewpoint. Vkara opened doors to a deeper understanding of self and a greater connection with Spirit. I am much more aware of my energy's impact in creating and changing my environment. I can truly say that I was enlightened through my connection with Vkara.
~ Michael Lopez, COO– Premier Enterprise Solutions

Vkara is a consummate professional who other professionals in the Coaching and Change business seek out. After working with Vkara I have been able to progress in the business world to an executive leadership role. Her perspectives are unique and challenging. There is no doubt that she is a true professional who can incorporate adventures to bring out strengths in people. I will say her work is life changing.
~Amy Fariss, Founder and CEO The Cortina Group and former V.P of H.R. at Quintiles Inc.

When Vkara shows up – things happen!
~ Pastor Miriam Niles – Senior Pastor RLTC

Contact information:
- MysticTREK.com
- MysticTreK@live.com
- Like Mystic Trek on Face Book
- Follow 'Mystic Trekker' on Twitter and 'mystictrekker' on Instagram

CHAPTER 4

THE SECRET POWER OF PERSEVERANCE

BY V. KRISHNA LAKKINENI

Your life can be more meaningful when you observe and learn from the nature. Always remember that the human race took an extraordinary journey to be where it is today. I believe we are born to live an amazing life filled with joy, peace and happiness. Here is my contribution to share some of the secrets that I learned so far in this life's journey.

Currently I live in Canada, immigrated here in 2008. By applying some of the life's lessons I founded a successful digital marketing agency. In 2012, I was recognized as an "Entrepreneur of the Year" at the Chamber of Commerce Business Excellence awards. We help clients with innovative, strategic digital marketing solutions that deliver results.

How did I get here?

Every incident leaves a memory. Some of these memories are sweet and some leave scars. But every incident teaches you something new. Each helps you to develop a belief. Some of the incidents in my life helped to shape my belief system around truth, integrity, trust, time management, and survival in life.

SEEK TRUTH – BREAK THE RULES OF LIVING

Question everything to seek the truth. Truth always prevails once you develop a sense to observe and learn. Seek truth; don't let others' beliefs limit you to see the full potential.

My childhood taught me so many lessons that some people didn't get an opportunity to learn in their lifetime. The biggest lesson I learned is that parents, friends and society impose "rules of living" on you. Most often, the perceptions set by others for you always lead to same outcomes. They can be cultural beliefs or family beliefs. If you want spectacular results in life, you need to think extraordinary – outside of the ordinary. In India, we have a caste system where you are supposed to do the duties assigned to your caste. However, I was fortunate enough to have a family that chose to do what's best for their kids rather than what's expected of their society.

I feel my success had its first stone laid many years even before I was born. My paternal grandfather felt education was the only way that gets us out of the poverty. Later on, my father continued the tradition to ensure we got educated well to survive in a modern society. I still remember his words, Wisdom and knowledge cannot be stolen! It allows you to live with dignity and earn respect in the society. My mom is a housewife and very supportive of my dad's vision and goals for the family. My dad is a school teacher and wanted me to become a teacher. However, I had a bigger dream, "A dream to help people." Later on, I realized that I especially like to change the lives of children who go through slavery, terrorism and sex trafficking. I felt it's important to be a business person and more importantly to be a leader to help people. So I became an entrepreneur to employee a few people and to help our clients where they can provide jobs to more people. Still, to date I am on a quest to fulfill my dreams; it only happened because of conscientious soul searching for truth. By breaking the rule of living I found my own purpose in life.

BELIEVE YOUR SUCCESS IS INEVITABLE

Overcome the many challenges and unknown forces that may hinder success. Don't let circumstances determine the outcome of your future. Stay focused and never give up. When you seek success, adopt the plan: "metamorphosis – like a butterfly."

My spiritual side definitely came from the maternal side of my family. It helped me to get closer to "my true inner self." I developed a sense of meaning to life at an early age. I still remember this beautiful memory of watching the birth of butterflies. A complicated process of an egg turned into a cocoon and then the metamorphosis into a butterfly. The larva had to eat so many green leaves before it goes into hibernation and sustain all the natural forces. I have observed that not every caterpillar hatched and turned into a butterfly. The pods are beautiful when the morning dew drops reflects rainbows from sunlight – definitely a jaw-dropping scenery. You are looking at hundreds of these pods hanging from the tree. When the baby butterflies were hatching out of the cocoons, I once tried to help them to fly out of the shell, but soon I realized that they take time to dry and expand their wings before they can move on to their next journey. I interpreted our lives are very similar: "we need to believe in our own strengths to create life." One journey after another we live on. You have a choice – to live through all the hassles and complete the learning cycle you meant to go through to fulfill your dreams, or give up and blame circumstances for your misfortune.

Observing butterflies taught me how to be successful and never give up. Our life is pre-destined and meant to follow its own cycle. What we are supposed to do is to find our inner purpose to follow this cycle.

USE FORGIVENESS AND FEAR AS YOUR STRENGTH TO WIN

Recognize those moments where you hurt someone's feelings or when you were unkind, either to your own parents or any living creatures – recognize this and ask their forgiveness. It helps you to be at peace and build strength.

Fortunately, I developed a good memory that allowed me to connect back to my past at many levels. This allowed me to overcome fear and to be kind. My earliest memory was a fearful one. I used to dream about a king cobra hanging from a rope; we had a lot of king cobras lurking around all the time. My mom later told me that it was an actual incident that happened when I was a month-old child. Once I knew what it was, my fear lifted as I now know the cause of the fear and nothing can harm me and the incident was from the past. Recognizing various incidents from my past allowed me to face fear and I used it in developing my strength. Since I lived in a village where there were many poisonous snakes, I have witnessed the birth of tens of eggs hatched at the same time. Little baby snakes tried to get into our house, it scared me. I used a bamboo staff to kill a few and push some away into the wild. I was an innocent child, but however, it caused me grief. By forgiving myself and asking the little animals for forgiveness helped me to relax and to be at peace.

Over the years, I developed natural instincts to face the fear and used it to win over difficult circumstances.

PAIN IS INEVITABLE WHEN YOU SEEK SUCCESS

Push yourself to the limits; test and hone your skills to become the best in the industry. Once you develop certain skills they never go away, but you need to sharpen them from time to time.

Fortunately, my parents were my first mentors and there were many in the later stages of my life. My dad, being a teacher, had high expectations of me. He pushed me to the limit so many times; there were occasions where I couldn't take it any longer. My mom always consoled me, but also she wanted to make sure I grew up to be good citizen. I was bitter about my situation, but it developed my passion to survive and live. I was fearful that I might not have a comfortable life with basic necessities. However, I survived, and this lead me to believe pain is inevitable when you seek greater success. The more the pain means the greater the success.

I was homeless for a short period, living with few necessities in life, I developed an attitude that no matter what, I could survive. We all have a choice, either you will be part of a herd or be successful and lead a herd. Still, to date I always leave safe harbour to experiment and challenge my intuition to come up with better solutions.

TIME IS PRECIOUS, USE IT WISELY TO BE MORE PRODUCTIVE

Allocate at least an hour a day to organize your life. Organize various daily tasks at hand and allocate sometime for future planning. Complete tasks according to your passion in the order of most important to least important.

My dad started his career earning $8 dollars a month as a school teacher. In those days, I was frustrated for not getting basic necessities like clothes, books or a decent pen. I couldn't afford to buy new notebooks, so I used to scrounge blank pages from senior students. I would stitch them together the way I like to make it work. Later on in life, this mentality helped me to think out of the box. It allows me to use what's at hand to solve a problem. In business, you have to make quick decisions.

Irrespective of my childhood circumstances, I was happy, I was fortunate to have a place where our family of five could live, eat a good meal and hang out with my friends when my dad was not around. He valued time so much that I learned at an early stage that every second in the past is gone forever. I now choose to be very careful with how I spend my time. I'm not sure what the next moment in the future can bring. I only know for sure about the current moment. Developing a belief is one thing, but maintaining it with the same discipline throughout the years helped me to refine it to achieve success.

Time is a precious commodity, but not money. You can earn money when you have time. How you organize your day to be productive every minute is up to you. Some of the challenges you may face include how you organize your day so you are able to spare time for meetings, work, your family and for your networking events.

TAKE RISKS TO ACHIEVE SUCCESS

Be creative and take risks – think innovatively to create your own life. There are many hidden opportunities, find them wisely.

I found my passion in entrepreneurship, technology and marketing. I aligned my goals with my passion. My passion has been transformed over the years. When I was an eight-year-old, it was about getting nutritional food, nice clean clothes and a pen. I have a fondness for pens, especially ink pens that you can dip and write. During my childhood, fountain pens were expensive and out of reach for me. I used to pick up feathers; I think they were vulture feathers. I would clean them and dip them in ink to write. That was a lot of fun. I've made candles out of wax collected from the bee hives. It's adventurous as there was no protection from the bees. You smoke the hive and run for your life or find a hive that's barren. However, there was a greater chance of finding sweet honey when we took the risk.

When I need peace, I used to sit on the banks of a creek that flowed into a pond. I've observed a school of fish, big and small, trying to swim upstream. The sun's reflection on the scales created a beautiful silver reflection I could never forget. There were cranes eagerly waiting to prey on the fish. However, many fish made it upstream. These observations allowed me to take bigger risks and gave me confidence that I can create what I want in my life. There are many incidents like this that built my confidence, and made me feel like the issues I am facing could be solved. When you can't have "X" you can always fill the emptiness with a "Y". I call them hidden opportunities, find them wisely.

FIND MENTORS – SEEK WISDOM FROM TRUE MENTORS

Show kindness and compassion where you can. It allows people to offer the same to others. Often it finds its way back to you.

When I was 17, getting through the university was my purpose. And then finding a job, and then getting married and having kids once you were settled. Indian culture has a notion of getting settled before you can get married. Working through the university helped me to graduate with distinction, which I am always grateful for all my professors and my family. I dreamed about living abroad where I could have a better job and provide a better life for my children. It was a difficult decision to make, but I had to make a tough choice for the future of my children and generations to come.

After graduation one of my professors offered a generous donation to sponsor my education in England. This changed my life forever; it laid a foundation for the next level of success. His words still echo in my ears, "I believe in you, in your strength to accomplish something much better." Later on in life, I continue the gratitude towards other students or people in need.

Mentors help you move forward with your vision. They help you get closer to your purpose by providing the wisdom.

ORGANIZED PERSISTENCE PAYS OFF – ENJOY THE PERKS

Be persistent with your vision; however, you must know that everything needs to be balanced. Take a moment to self-check your vitals for the day.

I used to be kind and I still am with people in my life. I got bullied at school many times, I'm sure it happened to every kid that went to school at some point. I was picked on in many occasions by other kids, or who made me sit on the bench in sports. I tried to play with them at every available occasion and made sure to ask them to play in the team rather than sitting on the bench. I was persistent until they accepted me into the game to play. I wasn't the best player, but soon they realized that I gave what it takes for the team.

To this day, I practice persistence in growing my business. What kept me going was my hard work and my eagerness to win. There were at least ten other agencies of various sizes when I started my agency. However, working a few extra hours a day I thought I could catch up. I sure did in a couple of years. But the downfall was I wasn't taking enough breaks, which had an effect on my health and my longevity working at the office. I decided to take regular breaks and diversify our clients to allow some fun while working. I learned to be persistent to achieve goals in life. However, everything needs a balance, like yin and yang.

Another important lesson I learned is that by celebrating our completed projects, this helps us to preserve the persistence.

Be relentless and enjoy the ride!

About Krishna

V. Krishna Lakkineni hailed from a small village in India. He was born with a desire to get out of the poverty struggles and lack of basic necessities made him work harder and made him hungry to achieve something better not just for him, but for his future family and generations to come. A ten-year-old's thoughts of having lots of money to solve these problems soon vanished. He soon realized there is something more than money—a higher purpose, one that drives every one of us to reach our goals. His self-discoveries lead him to find the inner passion to help others. He fulfills their dreams through mentoring, by giving and by showing compassion and love.

Through hard work, dedication and continuing education, he developed a unique skill set in the digital marketing industry where having a both analytical (left brain) and creative, imaginary (right brain) approach always lead to best quality projects.

He currently leads a great team of talented technologists, designers and strategists at ROI Media Works. Krishna has over 15 years of experience working in the ever-changing digital marketing world. Being analytical, as well as being an entrepreneur, programmer and a marketer, he has developed a unique yet strategic skill set where he sets the bar high. He had considerable experience working on Fortune 500 companies' digital marketing projects in an agency environment.

Krishna Lakkineni likes to excel in everything he does, and has built an agency that is closely associated with his beliefs:

*Be the best you can be and let the rest happen
naturally; let your intuition guide you.*

As a leader, he thrives in providing the best possible digital marketing solutions to ROI Media Works' clients no matter how big or small. Collectively, his team has received various industry awards –including a keystone marketing project award.

Krishna is also a Rotarian, volunteers in the community, and works on various non-profit projects where passion meets purpose. There are lot of other skills he developed over the time by observing nature and studying the intellect of others.

His intention to share these secrets is not for fame, but a mere attempt to prove that anything can be possible. His purpose is to identify and change the lives of one million children in need, including those who suffered through the hardships of war, slavery and sex trafficking. He is hoping to connect with like-minded people to lead the change in our society to protect our future generations – irrespective of their gender, nationality or social status.

You can find more of his tips at: www.lakkineni.com.

You can follow him on social networks for a regular dose of inspiration:
- LinkedIn: https://www.linkedin.com/in/klakkineni
- Instagram: https://www.instagram.com/krishna_lakkineni_/
- Facebook: https://www.facebook.com/klakkineni
- Twitter: https://twitter.com/lakkineni
- Quora: https://www.quora.com/profile/Krishna-Lakkineni

CHAPTER 5

ALIGN FOR IMPACT

BY CYNTHIA MILLS,
FASAE, CAE, CMC, CPC, CCRC

Five decades of life. Three decades of business.
One foundational truth – *Align for impact.*

My family loved camping – time together, nature walks, campfires, fishing, friends, and the freedom of wandering back roads. Readying for our next adventure, Dad would inch the truck backwards towards the trailer's hitch, while Mom guided him a little to the left and a little to the right. With eyes locked on lining up that metal ball, partnership flourished, dents were avoided, and we were speedily on our way. Frequently, I watched Dad's ability tested as he coaxed our trailer into a campsite between a tree obstacle course, angling the truck in puzzling directions to perfectly align our weekend home. When Mom and Dad were functioning from full partnership, his skills were operating at peak performance, goals were clear, roles were assigned, and their communication was unobstructed; our preparations were seamless, execution was perfect, and joy from being together was sweetened.

For several years, a campground was our summer home. With a stunning waterfall, inviting swimming lake, Saturday night dances, hayrides, and loads of friends, it was high-impact family time. My parents bartered a campsite in return for running weekend recreation events and Dad's Sunday preaching. Camping was in alignment with our values, interests, and finances; and good stewardship benefited all. Years later, the owners' children carry on the traditions with Sunday services, wholesome family fun, and community building – continuing high impact experiences throughout the decades. My parents' lifelong choices to remain in step with their values and callings created high impact for our family and wore a Sherpa's path for others to follow that is still impacting thousands of people; many whom they never met.

Alignment is a discipline and practice that requires clarity on the desired outcome, self-awareness, patience, consistency, persistence, sacrifice at times, skill, boundary identification, and a little guiding hand from others. We're pulled into early contemplation from childhood when adults begin asking the dreaded, "What do you want to be when you grow up?" They are really asking us, "With what jobs do your talents and interests align?" A better question is, "*Who* do you want to be?" - which points us to, "How do you want to have impact throughout your life, upon whom or what, and to what extent?" Therefore, "With what and whom should you align, and why?" With these answers, we can design our lives and identify behaviors and actions that, when consistently practiced, leverage our impact to unprecedented heights. Failure to do so accelerates us like an untethered elevator, plummeting to the depths of chaos; leaving us floundering to avoid the abyss of a disjointed journey.

If there is one question that plagues adults throughout their lives, it's a version of, "Did I make the right choice?" – which leads to, "Is there something else I want to do?" "What if I've gotten my life wrong?" There is nothing more traumatic than not recognizing yourself – in the choices you've made, the jobs you've taken, the family you do or don't have, and the God you do or don't serve. In those crisis moments, we see our misalignment and our failure to create the maximum positive impact for others and ourselves. That culmination usually requires taking what feels like the biggest risks in life and making the deepest sacrifices to dramatically alter our course and increase our impact.

The agony most often heard from CEOs, executives, young professionals, wives, mothers, fathers, and husbands is a fear of letting go of the very entrapment causing the misalignment. Their pain is palpable and yet, oddly known and comfortable. It manifests in illness, acting out behaviors, depression, anxiety, broken relationships, job failures, and despair. The irony is that it goes beyond getting the same thing from continuing to do the same thing.[1] It becomes a deliberate choice to stay frozen and not create impact. In that moment of recognition, no one else

1. Attribution to Albert Einstein, though unconfirmed, "The definition of insanity: doing the same thing over and over again, expecting different results."

can be blamed for your misalignment. If not altered, you are now doing it to yourself, choosing inertia. When paralysis is replaced by stepping towards unknown territory that magnetically resonates with our talents, values, and calling, it is staggering how quickly personal healing shows up. . . voices get lighter. . . possibility appears. . . new people enter lives. . . resources show up. . . energy is magnified. . . the road map unfolds. . . light replaces darkness. . . new lives are created.

We can mistake this journey to alignment as only personal, perceiving that it's about an individual finding their reason for existence or intersection with their passion. Transforming lives is one outcome of aligning for impact, and it can be powerful. However, it's just as relevant for values-driven companies and organizations when precisely aligned with vision, resources, complementary people, and skilled execution. The experience is similar, both positively and negatively.

Much has been written about Southwest Airline's alignment, marketplace disruption, and enduring success. Fueling employees' devotion, passengers' enthusiasm, and financial fruits, Southwest is a true illustration of positive alignment of vision, values, leadership, behavior, and rewards for all parties - employees, stockholders, and customers. The resulting impact was leveraged exponentially, magnified, and *shared*!

More recently, alleged improprieties at a corporation are unfolding. It appears that the value of greed may have superseded integrity; that making the numbers was more important than treating employees and customers with respect and honesty. The influence of this apparent corporate culture has had great negative impact via media coverage, lost jobs, brand impact, and uncertainty. Recovery is hard after a trustbuster of this magnitude. Light shone upon core operations and leadership may indicate values, beliefs, behaviors, and actions showed up in a way that may be out of alignment with laws and customer expectations. It matters with what you are aligned. Alignment for impact is not an insurance policy for positive results, without ascertaining carefully with what you associate. It matters with whom you do business and how you choose to conduct it.

Early days as the tree care industry's CEO validated the business owners were folks with whom my parents would want me to associate; primarily family-owned businesses, from a billion-dollar corporation to small operations – God, family, and apple pie. Smart, successful leaders, they performed physics calculations in their heads, protected commercial properties and people's homes, helped keep the lights on, provided jobs, and took care of the one renewable resource we have in this world.

There was opportunity to exponentially increase their impact from accredited businesses to certified safety professionals to expanded marketplaces to responsible regulation to transforming the industry for the next century. The Board, the members, and the staff took it on. Seventeen years later, their association has an even higher stature with more staff and representatives nationwide and fabulous leadership. Their coffers are full. They have saved lives. They take pride in their professional gifts, the protection and beautification they provide, their employees' successes, and their contributions to the world. They are in alignment with their transformational vision, core values, purpose, how their companies do business, and how their association represents and supports them. They are aligned for maximum positive *impact*.

This state does not appear in a flash, because you decide that you or your company will seek alignment and desire to have greater impact. It requires concerted effort and commitment to make sure the components are in place to design the environment in which it can flourish. When assessment first begins, it is not unusual to start from a slightly arrogant assumption that we are already aligned, and just need to tweak it a little for more impact. However, circumstances are often not as anticipated and require significant attention and dedication to redesign. In fact, as we commit to align for impact, there can be a momentary personal or company breakdown when reality hits that necessitates outside expertise to navigate.

Align for impact *is* the big secret, both personally and for companies and organizations. Below are starting points to begin your walk from both perspectives.

If you are undertaking this assessment solely for yourself, there are others with whom you must share your new understandings and from whom you will need support. Some will not understand your new behaviors and will question why you are walking away from what they thought was your clear path.

Examination to reveal clarity for impact must include honest self-awareness, patience when the journey is longer than anticipated, consistency in our efforts, persistence towards the greatest impact, unexpected sacrifice at times, enhanced skill, boundary identification, and a little guiding hand from others who possess needed proficiency. Experts in facilitating this work can be helpful in nurturing you or your organization through some of the painful admissions, authoring new plans, encouraging you through the sacrifices, guiding you through implementation, recruiting others to be partners, and helping you create your new stories so you can communicate, communicate, and communicate some more.

It takes an average of seven times for new content to stick. If your company is altering its message for impact, who do you think must get it first - your employees or your customers? Your employees! If they don't internalize the message, it doesn't get passed on to marketing, emphasized in collaboration, incorporated into how performance is measured, utilized in budgeting decisions, included on strategic agendas, and of course, communicated to your customers. Your alignment matters in the fabric of your culture. Its texture, dye quality, colors, thread count, durability, and story are all revealed in how you execute on your alignment. Culture will determine the paucity or abundance of your impact.

Ultimately, we seek:

I. You *being* everything for which you were created and making your greatest positive life impact, while avoiding wasted time, resources, and distractions.

II. Your company or organization *living* a vision of significance, emboldening its mission, and aligning values, culture, and capacity to replicate maximum positive impact in perpetuity.

When these conditions exist, frustration is diminished, collaboration is natural, innovation bursts forth, processes support ideas, capacity multiplies, engagement accelerates, relevance is obvious, and value is evident. In this state, people, ideas, and impact integrate at unparalleled rates.

12 STEPS TO PERSONAL ALIGNMENT FOR IMPACT

Consider these twelve steps to maximize your personal alignment, contribute your greatest positive life impact, and *be* everything for which you were created.

1. I feel most alive when: _ _ _

2. I believe my gifts and talents are: _ _ _

   2a. Others compliment me on these attributes, skills, and abilities: _ _ _

3. My core values are: Personally: _ _ _ Professionally: _ _ _

   If they differ, I know why: _ _ _

4. My personal mission statement (purpose in life) is: _ _ _

5. My vision for my life is: _ _ _

6. I could increase my vision's impact by: _ _ _

7. I am out of alignment in these ways: _ _ _

8. Corrective steps I am willing to take over the next week, month, quarters, and year are: _ _ _

9. I allow myself to provide negative self-talk in these areas, which creates barriers to my impact: _ _ _

10. I need this person/these people as champions for my vision's ultimate impact: _ _ _

11. My resources to create my greatest impact are (time, people, money, prayer): _ _ _

12. When I die, my obituary will say, "_____'s life impact was ____."

12 STEPS TO COMPANY AND ORGANIZATION ALIGNMENT FOR IMPACT

To replicate maximum positive impact in perpetuity, consider these twelve steps to visions of significance, emboldened missions, and aligned values, culture, and capacity.

1. Without looking at any document, can you, the leader, share the clear vision, mission, and values statements by which decisions are made and to which employees can point as they execute daily? Can your employees share it as well?

   If the company's direction is clear, are you setting the example by walking the talk, easily integrating strategic impact language into every dialogue?

2. How do our employees demonstrate our values daily with our customers?

   Do employees know our intentional discipline of how we deliver on our promises?

3. How do leadership, governance, advertising, performance reviews, policies, budgets, behaviors, rewards, and employee and customer experiences align with our core beliefs?

   Are we creating a culture from our strategic expectations and values that is woven into our corporate soul?

4. When we have to make difficult decisions, to what do we turn first - the bottom line, stockholders, stakeholders, the competition, vision/ mission, values, strategy, our people, evaluation and adjustment, or innovation?

   Are we consistent with the drivers behind how we do business so that we remain relevant and sustainable for the long-term, or do we slide to lesser goals and reduced impact during tough times?

5. During our most robust periods, the way that we share our success with our customers and our employees can be witnessed by...?

   Is impact defined just by our bottom line, or can we detail how we are responsible to our people, our community, and those to whom our success can be attributed?

6. Is our strategic plan the guide for our owner/board meetings and the major topic for our leadership team's meetings?

   Are we constantly viewing our present and future through the lens of our intended outcomes' impact, or are we caught up in the busyness of "doing," without knowing what the diversions cost us?

7. Do we conduct at least one annual strategic session to refresh our plans, select our focus for the coming year, and responsibly use our capacity?

   Are we disciplined in our pursuit of impact, celebrating our achievements, targeting the next logical steps to leverage our strategy, and keeping clarity and communication at the forefront of our interactions with employees?

8. How do our employees demonstrate to us regularly that they are focused on the impact we are attempting to achieve?

   Without having a meeting, can I see our vision coming to life through the daily actions of our employees?

9. How do we respond culturally to an employee or a customer who calls us out on misalignment or our failures to live up to our values or customer promises?

   Do our employees point out where we are falling short, help us to improve, and take pride in our corporate culture to seek impact?

10. What is the greatest impact we can complete in the next year?

    Do we know how to set short-term wins to keep the momentum toward ultimate impact going; creating a celebratory culture for employees and customers?

11. What level of impact could set us apart from our competitors?

    Have we done our homework to ascertain what relevance means in relationship to our core competencies?

12. Since any company can set and achieve a financial target, for what do we want to be remembered?

    What problem can we solve that creates unforgettable impact?

One foundational truth – ***Align for impact.***
Will yours be positive, negative, or unnoticed?

About Cynthia

Cynthia Mills is Founder, President & CEO of The Leaders' Haven, a consultancy partnering with clients to align for impact and exceed expectations.

Transformation Architect: An award-winning national and international CEO, Cynthia designs transformational and sustainable impact in complex companies and organizations as business strategist, succession planning and transition facilitator, board consultant, leadership development catalyst, executive coach, change management guide, and speaker. Serving a diverse client portfolio, Cynthia brings depth and unique perspective to each engagement, matching culture and enhancing corporate soul for relevance in business and industry, finance, energy, healthcare, co-op, legal, retail, agriculture, senior living, real estate, environmental, publishing, media, transportation, construction, education, entertainment, safety, philanthropy, and faith sectors.

Leader Cultivator: On her journey from student government representative to international CEO and consultant, Cynthia parlayed her expertise building strategy, people, and teams into lauded designer of corporate leadership programs and executive coach. As New England College adjunct faculty, Cynthia also developed curricula and taught strategic planning and policy, the dynamics of governance, and thesis preparation to master's degree candidates.

World Citizen: A small town girl with big dreams, Cynthia has been blessed to live and speak abroad, represent organizations in Asia, Europe, Scandinavia, the UK, Mexico, Canada, Bermuda, the Caribbean, and the U.S.; and lead diverse teams, engaging with professionals globally. Her suitcase stays partially packed, ready to go.

Eternal Student: Cynthia holds an MA from the University of York, England, earned as a Rotary International Ambassador Scholar, and was purported to be the first U.S. southern student to attend, after earning a dual BA from Queens College as a Presidential Scholar. She is a member of the Institute of Management Consultants, Association of Charlotte Area Consultants, International Coach Federation, International Coaching Council, American Society of Association Executives, Association Executives of North Carolina, Georgia Society of Association Executives, and Strathmore Who's Who Worldwide. Cynthia is certified as a Master Coach, Professional Coach, Christian Coach, and Association Executive.

Peer Recognition: Strathmore *Who's Who Worldwide* selected Cynthia as Professional of the Year in Consulting, Coaching and Professional Development. Business Leader Media named her Business Leader Woman Extraordinaire. TCIA recognized Cynthia's

CEO leadership twice with The Chair's Award. Queens College identified her as one of Ten Who Make a Difference and bestowed the Algernon Sydney Sullivan Award. ASAE named Cynthia a Fellow, granted to less than 1% of the profession, and colleagues subsequently elected her Fellows Chair. GSAE honored her with the Clifford Clarke Award, President's Award, 90 Movers & Shakers, and Lifetime Honorary Membership. Cynthia was also named the inaugural Association Executive of the Year by Southeastern Association Executive Magazine.

Author: *The Big Secret* is Cynthia's fourth book, following *CEOs First 90 Days: Breathing Tips for the Other End of the Fire Hose* and *The Empty Front Porch: Soul Sittin' to Design Your porch to Porch Plan.* She is also a co-author of *The Female Factor: A Confidence Guide for Women.*

To align for impact and exceed expectations, you can reach the author at:
- CynthiaMills@TheLeadersHaven.com
- www.TheLeadersHaven.com
- www.twitter.com/TheLeadersHaven
- www.linkedin.com/in/leadershavenceo

CHAPTER 6

THE FORTUNE IS IN THE FOLLOW-UP

BY MELANIE GAMBLE

If you want to create meaningful relationships and experience opportunity, be aware and engaged with the world around you.

Most people do not recognize how much opportunity they miss as they go about their daily activities. There is always a fire to put out or a problem to solve. The to-do list is never completed. This leads to having a narrow vision of what must be done, which often surpasses the potential of what could be. I'm talking about opportunity, and making it happen, not just hoping that you stumble into it. Remember, opportunity is only a person away and the best way to get it is by *FOLLOWING UP!*

For starters, how is "follow-up" defined? This is the way I view it in the work I do and the way I choose to navigate both my personal and professional life:

Follow-up is contact that comes from a genuine place of desire to create value for others by being of service to them. Through focusing on what you can offer others, the reciprocating benefits happen in an authentic, highly relevant manner.

With my career of real estate, the follow-up is essential. You don't close deals without it, much less educate consumers on what they can expect— from the market and from their Realtor®. It doesn't matter if they are buying a home or selling their home, or perhaps both. To cement the importance of follow-up by my definition, consider this:

According to 2016 information from the NAR, 72% of recent sellers contacted only one agent before finding the right agent they worked with to sell their home. The number rises up to 77% for those sellers that are thirty-five years and younger.

Statistics like this tell us that if we don't provide value and service to as many people as we can upfront, our chances of just happening to be that first person in line for that seller are slim. There are a lot of agents out there. However, if we offer value and meaning through follow-up, we will be remembered and sought out. It's a smarter way for EVERYONE to do business, not just Realtors®, and what I'm sharing is for every professional who wants to develop critical skills for success, as well as the ability to cultivate meaningful relationships in their lives.

OUR DAILY EXPERIENCES

At the hub of both our business lives and personal lives are our interactions with other people. We rely on them and they are what create the experiences of our lives.

Think of how you spend your time in a given day. I'm not talking about your schedule, *per se*, but the value you give to your time and others when you are face-to-face with them. Do you give your full attention or glance at the time, thinking about what you have to do next? Despite being busy—something most people appreciate, as they are too—what if you began thinking about your interaction with that person in a more profound way?

What if that "great opportunity" was just one person away?

Could that person in front of you be "the one" who knows someone that can change your life in an exciting and positive way? Let's assume that they could. Now ask yourself this: did you give them your genuine self and participate in creating a connection that would make you worthy of that referral, recommendation, or introduction? The right follow-up will make you that person, because you are genuine and of service. That's service, not "self-service"!

A life-changing opportunity may be only a single connection away.

Today's world is a social media-driven world, which means that it's harder to make connections that are genuine and in which you will be a stand-out. Plus, we're all so busy with work and when we're not working, we often struggle to maintain a great balance between our family time and our friend time, not to mention a little necessary and precious "me time." The thought of adding more people into that mix can seem impossible, maybe even improbable. This leaves ones question.

How do you create a meaningful connection to others with everything going on in your life?

Our personal and professional lives demand meaning, and it's in the follow-up that we can find it, and that's what I'm so excited to share insight on. Furthermore, once we focus on creating thoughtful connections life can become easier, the way we spend our time is shifted, and our results soar to exciting new levels...and opportunities!

CREATING CONNECTIONS: THERE IS A STRATEGY FOR EVERYONE

As you reflect on your life, think about how many meaningful relationships you already have. Then imagine the potential of what you could do if you had even one more...

A concept that I love that shows how a single person can potentially positively impact many thousands of people stems from doing one thing every day: meet three new people. Reach out to someone with genuine intent. Maybe there's a connection and synergy there or maybe not. That's okay. We aren't meant to connect with everyone we meet. However, our odds of developing rapport and relationships with people we can offer value to, and who also offer value to us, goes up considerably. Just imagine...if you started this concept when you were five—the age where they say we begin to remember those we meet better—and lived to the ripe age of eighty, we'd be able to create enough connections that we could fill nearly an 80,000 person stadium. There is definitely at least one opportunity in that stadium that you would not have had otherwise... And most likely, many more than one!

Keep in mind, with social media these touches do not have to always start face-to-face, either. This is brilliant, because it opens up opportunity for those who may be hesitant about bolder social engagement. One of the most wonderful things about social media is that we can engage in meaningful relationship building and conversation through sharing our appropriate, professional insights and opinions, all while not feeling invasive.

Then there are the people we've known in our lives…those that drifted away or we lost touch with:

Keeping up with where our contacts are used to be an intensive process—mail or telephone calls. I remember my big old rolodex, filled with card after card of contacts. Then it transitioned to business cards. The problem was that if someone moved or changed phone numbers, they were very hard to track down if you weren't in "constant contact." Today's technology allows me to have 3,000 contacts at my disposal—just in my phone, and with social media, I can track people down more easily.

There's one story that I want to share with you to demonstrate the point. I grew up with and went to school with Roy Jones, Jr., the Olympic boxer and now actor, commentator, etc. He was a nice guy, we'd say hi in the halls, and then we all graduated, each going our separate ways. We lost contact, each pursuing our own goals. A few years ago I happened to run into him at the airport with my kids, and I was so excited to be able to go up to him and say "hi" and have my kids get their picture taken with him—it was especially a thrill for my middle son who is very passionate about sports. It was great to have that opportunity, but the entire time I thought: *how much cooler would it have been if I'd kept that friendship all the while; that it still existed and we could give each other a call or send a message congratulating each other on their achievements.*

It isn't easy to keep up with those connections and most certainly, when you do catch up it has to be genuine and natural—not just a sales pitch for something or a "let's talk about me, me, me" encounter.

Let me share what happened when I recently finally made a connection with someone I'd lost contact with after college. We'd been great friends and roommates and then eventually adult life happened, we grew apart as we each began our own journeys. We ended up seeing each other at a conference—twenty years later—and were shocked to realize that we lived in the same area. We talked and made the promise that we'd get together soon for coffee and catch-up. It kept getting put off, never working, and being pushed back for months (five), but finally, we did it! We got together and it was so wonderful. There were a lot of things that we had in common and ways in which we could both be of value to each other, friendship aside. She was a new entrepreneur, recently having left the work force, and I had insights to offer her about being an entrepreneur from my twenty plus years of experience. Some of the things she had to offer me were just what I needed, too. That conversation ended with a win/win. We reconnected, it was authentic and invigorating. Now that's powerful!

Regardless of how we earn a living, we can do so better through establishing good connections with others. Not every opportunity has to be made from scratch, and simply following up with people and giving them a bit of your focused attention is very effective.

SOWING WHAT YOU SEEK

It's easy to say what you want and expect, but achievement requires action.

Here's a tough question: What are you willing to do to get what you say you want?

As a coach and mentor with a passion for helping women to lead empowered lives, I must address this significant question first. It comes before:

- Learning how to effectively follow-up
- Learning everything you need to know
- Understanding how to schedule out your day

Think of a doctor. Do they go from a four-year degree to working as a resident in a hospital? No, it takes many years of intensive focus for them to reach that point. If they don't want it, it's likely not going to work, because they are not willing to put in the time it requires. The same is true for any career or ambition that you may have.

Coaching and mentoring in real estate is something I do quite often. In one of my more recent experiences I was working with a woman who'd had a successful corporate executive career, but had decided to change careers to be a full time Realtor® and try her hand at success. We began to go through all the details to create a success plan. I asked how much she needed to make. She answered that she needed to make $100K in order to maintain the same lifestyle she had. It was a starting point, and from there we talked about the market she wanted to serve. It was homes that were in the $300K and above price range. From there, we broke it down and determined how many people she would need to touch in order to have a chance at success.

You have to walk people through what they want and what that involves— exactly. It's a more precise methodology than you might think.

In this case, she needed to honestly determine if she was:

- **Willing** to get up at 5 AM every day to work out for an hour before getting ready for work and the kids off to school.
- **Agreeable** to being at the office by 7 AM to start planning her day.
- **Able** to schedule appointments for the day by 9 AM so she had the rest of the day available for reaching her goals.

AND

- **Committed** to doing this every day for as long as it took to reach her objective.

This makes for a long and intensive day. If your passion and commitment to your objective are not strong, you're not going to accomplish it. Not because you're a failure, but because you lacked the breadth of understanding necessary. What you want cannot be different than what you're willing to invest.

FOLLOW-UP AND LIFT-UP

I'm on a mission to expose the big secret: following up is necessary to avoid giving up.

The desire to add power to peoples' lives is a strong and powerful motivator for me. Through my businesses, motivational speaking platform, and coaching to help others garner meaningful success, I've been blessed with so many amazing relationships and connections in my life. It's always a wonderful day when I can call a professional relationship a friend, as well.

I'd like to leave you with two challenges, one personal and one professional: First, take a moment to reach out to someone you've lost contact with whom you always valued. Use it as an opportunity to learn about what they've been up to. Second, think of one interesting or impactful person that you've met that you'd like to learn more from. Reach out to them and get to know them better, find out what their "big secrets" to success are.

By participating in challenges such as this, that is how you learn and grow. And, of course, follow-up with a thank you!

About Melanie

Melanie Gamble is an author, speaker, real estate expert and entrepreneur. As the owner of two RE/MAX franchises and 212 Degrees Realty, LLC, Melanie's expertise has given the markets in Maryland, DC, and Virginia, highly-trained and committed Realtors® to help them experience success in the home buying and selling process.

Providing top-notch, personalized customer service and guaranteeing excellence are hallmarks of her work for every client. For her, helping people to own and keep their homes is not only a business endeavor but a personal passion and a spiritual mission. As a cancer survivor, Melanie is acutely aware of how precious life and time are for all of us; she seeks to help others make the most of what they are given.

A two-time graduate of Florida A&M University, Melanie holds a Bachelor's Degree in Criminal Justice and a Master's Degree in Public Administration. While in graduate school, Melanie became the first woman and youngest Executive Director of the Florida Conference of Black State Legislators. Her proudest moment came during the 1994 legislative session when she had the opportunity to work with the descendants of Rosewood. She lobbied exceptionally hard for the introduction and passage of the Rosewood bill, which awarded the descendants of Rosewood, FL over 3 million dollars in reparations.

Melanie is a John C. Maxwell Certified Coach, Teacher, and Speaker who is committed to working with a wide variety of women regardless of their age, race or socioeconomic status. In addition to her busy work life, she regularly volunteers at organizations dedicated to children, women and health, including Doctor's Community Hospital, Children's Miracle Network and her own non-profit, Esther's Closet, which donates new and gently used prom gowns and accessories to young women.

Melanie is author of the book, *Unintended Consequences* and she is co-author with renowned author and coach Jack Canfield in the book, *The Big Secret.*

When Melanie gets those rare, precious moments of "me time", she enjoys cozying up to a good book, shopping, and giving herself a little spa rejuvenation. She's eternally grateful to her husband Jay, who has always had the strength to allow her to shine and flourish, being a true partner and friend along the way. Melanie and Jay enjoy life with their three sons in Maryland.

CHAPTER 7

PEOPLE QUIT PEOPLE

BY MEGAN MCMANUS

In 2015, nearly a quarter of the workforce (33.4 million people) quit their job. I'm sure we all know at least one out of the 33.4 million that opted for a better job, higher pay or more flexibility. Heck, maybe that person was you.

Or perhaps you are counted in the 37% of workers who are considering leaving their job soon. I don't blame you. In fact, I'm right there with you. In the last 12 years, I've quit five jobs, three of them before I had a solid plan of what I was going to do next. All of them had one thing in common, and it's the same factor I believe played into a large majority of the 33 million cases above and it's no secret.

Before I dive in too deep, I feel the need to elaborate a bit. I'm a millennial. Go ahead and throw out your distaste for this generation. We're lazy, we don't focus, we lack work ethic, etc. I've heard it all and read all the books on how to manage us. Although our approach to getting the job done may be different, our reason for working and sticking with a company is no different than any other generation.

Let me take you on a journey first and then explain the one reason MOST employees say "I quit." My first job was mowing yards with my father and brother… a family business if you will. They started mowing when I was in grade school, and I helped by holding the garbage bags or bringing them water. Once I was old enough, I took over the mowing for my brother and ran alongside my dad trying to keep up with the 30 or so yards we took care of each month.

I made great money but it wasn't the most glamorous job, and my "boss" was a bit of a stickler for early mornings and a strict schedule. So, when our final mow of the season had concluded, I began looking for a part-time gig that would put money in my pocket and take me out of the Oklahoma heat. Dad wasn't the biggest fan of the decision. However, it was probably the best move for not only me, but our relationship. Working for family can be tough.

Next, I took up pushing drugs… legal drugs that is! I worked as a pharmacy tech for a mom-and-pop shop just minutes away from the university I was attending. Convenient…yes! Not only was it five minutes from all my classes, but the customers were great, I loved the two ladies I worked alongside, and the bosses wife was awesome. It wasn't the hardest job, but depending on the day, stress levels could escalate when the boss wasn't …umm…happy. It was easy to take it out on the techs, and when something went wrong, nine times out of 10 it was our fault.

Now, pharmacy tech was not a long-term career goal for me, but I would have happily stuck with the job for the duration of my college years without hesitation. Unfortunately, the boss and I didn't mesh well. I had feelings, and he didn't care about them. In the long run, it wasn't worth the stress. Luckily for me, I had an opportunity to become a student worker on campus and didn't think twice.

I know what you're thinking… student worker? Those students get paid to sit and study, right? I wish! Many students across campus had the opportunity to kick back, lounge in sweatpants and hoodies all while studying for their next exam or work on homework from the previous class. I, however, was selected to be a student worker for the University President (the pressure)!

Being a student worker was a great job. Not only was it 57 steps from door to door to my first class, but it was flexible with my schedule, paid well, the dress code wasn't too strict and nearly all the professors on campus knew I worked for the president. I even had one professor that would ask me to pass messages along to the president or be a bit more lax with me if I walked in a few minutes late. I'm not going to lie… it was nice.

In the beginning, I did your random student worker jobs from stuffing envelopes, making copies, running errands and the like, but when the President found out I was a graphic designer, the level of responsibility grew as did my position. I went from student work to the official graphic designer for the University where I began creating all printed material, signage, etc. for the entire campus. Although I had to move out of the President's office and move downstairs into Community Relations, the trade-off of taking on such an enormous responsibility while still a student was an incredible honor. I was in my element with the free reign to determine the brand for the university. If any department had a request for materials, they came to me – a sophomore graphic designer that was just a few months away from her associates. What was the president thinking?

This job allowed me to excel in the things I was good at and loved to do. I had the autonomy to do my job and do it well, until the new supervisor I was reporting to, decided to move on from the university. Within a few weeks, a younger gentleman stepped in to take over, and everything changed. The place I once spent extra hours, long nights and weekends working on university projects when I should have been studying became a place I dreaded going to. In less than six months, the entire team I worked with quit. When I turned in my two weeks notice, I was escorted out by campus security – the same campus security that was there to keep me safe (remember, I was still a student).

I struggled to figure out where I went wrong but knew my decision to quit would allow me to focus on bigger and better things going forward. That day I vowed never to stay in a position where I was so undervalued, unappreciated and unhappy. It didn't matter how much I loved what I did; I could always do great things elsewhere for people who appreciated it.

Are you starting to see a trend?

My senior year in college, I was presented with an internship opportunity with a government agency and was excited to try something new. Now this job wasn't as convenient as my other positions, but it did pay a bit more and offered the long-term ability to take on a full-time position when I graduated (definitely necessary as I'm not sure my parents want me living at home forever).

This job had a few more rules (as any government agency does), but it was just a means to an end. I was there to do a project, get it approved and move on to the next project. There was no interaction with others. I walked into a room with a handful of programmers that preferred the lights off and no conversation. I may have exchanged a small number of words with my supervisor on a daily basis and nothing more. "Hi, how are you?" doesn't keep me motivated to call this my long-term career.

I decided at the end of the internship, government work was not for me. It paid well, had great benefits, a ton of random holidays, but no one cared about me or appreciated what I could offer. And so, job #4 came and went.

Once I graduated from the University, I started job #5 and joined a local real estate company as a Marketing Coordinator. I was back in my element of doing what I loved with complete autonomy and flexibility. I was welcomed into this "family" with open arms as we all worked hard together to reach common goals.

Marketing was just my foot in the door as I thrived there taking on new challenges and responsibilities. I helped with operations, special projects and multiple random initiatives not even related to my job, but proud of the opportunity and honored to be the one entrusted to accomplish the goal.

After two short years with the company, I was presented with an opportunity to relocate to Dallas, Texas from Oklahoma. Now, I use the term "opportunity" lightly because it was presented "either I move, or lose my job." I enjoyed the responsibility; I was doing what I loved, and the people I worked with were great...what the heck! Dallas... here I come!

In Dallas, I began working for the owner's second company helping with branding, website creation, etc. It was a rocky road, but I built relationships with the new team and acquired new skills as I took on more responsibility.

Over the next few years, I learned more, gained confidence and produced results from nearly every project I took over. So, when a new position came open, I didn't hesitate and raised my hand for the opportunity to become a project manager for a new company concept, which involved running a team. Now, to be clear – I was still young and green when it came to managing or leading others, but I didn't believe it was out of line to be considered. You would have thought I said Bigfoot is real! The reaction from my supervisor was a gut check for sure.

I can hear his response now just as clear as the day it was said: "You can't even manage yourself, how are you going to manage others."

As you can probably take away from my earlier positions, I can tend to give up a bit too early but in this case I stayed and worked twice as hard. From an outsider looking in, I was leading the team in less than six months. I didn't have a title, rather, the flow of traffic when someone needed help, guidance or advice came my way every time.

You see, I knew what it was like to have leaders who never took the time to understand me. I didn't leave the jobs before because I hated what I was doing, rather I never had a leader that connected with me and where I wanted to go. So, I started doing the little things that mattered to those around me to see if in fact it makes a difference and it did.

I fell in love with the people.

There's a saying, "people don't care how much you know until they know how much you care" and it's 100% correct. I connected with each person, set expectations, built out goals and pushed them to levels of success they never thought possible. And I was more fulfilled in this role than any other position prior. I may have been great at graphic design, but this is where I was meant to be.

Unfortunately for me, my leader was not as connected. He drove the business based on money and investments vs. making time investments with his people. Although I was doing work that was more rewarding and I had bought into the vision of the company, I had not bought into my leader and who he was as a person.

I quit.

I could have named my salary; I could have owned part of the company and rather, I walked away from something I loved and built from scratch because of a person and nothing more.

I didn't quit the company. I quit a person.

The not-so-big secret as to why the 33.4 million individuals left their jobs in 2015… people quit people. If they tell you it's because of money, flexibility, benefits or greater opportunity, they are lying to you.

People quit people.

If you are a manager, leader, executive, company owner, I beg you to pay attention. An alarming 93% of senior managers are satisfied with both the organization and the job, yet 63% are seriously considering leaving their job in the coming months.

Nearly 68% of millennials are proud to work for their organization, yet 44% are seriously considering leaving their job. It's no surprise when you reflect on those who have left you as to why they left. The best part is you can do something about it before it's too late.

I have tested and developed for the past thirteen years a series of principles that are key to growing a team to grow the business. Here are five simple things you can do now to get connected with your people:

1. HAVE GENUINE AND CONSISTENT ONE-ON-ONES

Set aside time monthly, if not weekly, to connect with your people. A one-on-one should be their opportunity to talk about life, voice concerns, communicate feedback and strategize on goals. Allow 30 minutes but don't force it if it goes long. Everyone wants to be a part of something bigger and genuinely do something real or important. Ensure that you are giving open and honest feedback and building them up for the things they do well, and encouraging them on the things they can do better.

2. CREATE OPPORTUNITY AND GIVE AUTONOMY

Understand what makes each person on your team tick. Once you uncover their drive, create opportunities to excel. Even if a new position isn't available just yet, mini-projects can make just as big of an impact for an employee to take ownership and excel on a project. Once you create the opportunity, give them the authority and autonomy to accomplish the goal. Ownership, no matter how big, can make a significant impact.

3. LISTEN TO YOUR PEOPLE

It's important to truly listen to your people and understand their concerns, fears, and expectations to lead effectively. Feelings are always 100% legit for the individual who voices them. Listen, confirm you hear what they are saying and then work together to resolve their feelings or find a solution. Also know, feelings don't always need a solution.

4. PAINT THE VISION AND UPDATE OFTEN

It's important that your people are aligned and working towards a common goal. And no matter if you're the company owner or division leader, you must talk about the vision and give updates often. Ensuring everyone is on the same page leaves the confusion, guesswork, and assumptions out of the way (that often leads to unanswered questions and uneasiness amongst employees).

5. SELF-REFLECT AND BE HONEST

The most important thing to do is self-reflect on previous turnover and be honest about the reasons. Learning from what happened before may help you ensure it doesn't happen again. In any situation ask, "What could I have done differently?" and you'll be surprised at the answer and results.

I currently consult startup and small business owners in building their businesses around people. I also now manage two key divisions for one of the fastest-growing technology companies with the opportunity to lead millennials and baby boomers alike. My number one focus is making time investing in, challenging and empowering those on the team. It's hands down the most rewarding (and important) thing I do. The personnel have a direct impact on the success of the company, and it's my goal to have a direct bearing on their path to bigger dreams and brighter futures.

About Megan

Megan McManus helps businesses grow through the development and empowerment of their employees. Working in several different industries, Megan gravitated toward people and how a little time investment can go a long way. Megan's leadership in people helped grow a 3-times INC. 500/5000 business, and was a critical piece of making the largest transaction in real estate technology possible.

Megan's passion is centered around her philosophy that "people quit people." Her goal is to help entrepreneurs and leaders understand that people are the most critical piece of their growth and without time investment; there is no long-term business success. Megan has also created a hiring and recruiting process focused on "fit vs function" that helps ensure any company is bringing in the right people from the start.

Megan is a graduate of Cameron University. She has worked in the real estate space for 12+ years starting out designing and marketing then moved into running operations, hiring and business strategy. Currently, Megan is an executive with Commissions Inc., the fastest growing real estate technology company, where she is the General Manager of Appointments Inc. and the Vice President of Training. With her experience with rapid business growth and hiring strategies, Megan has shared the stage with some of the best small business entrepreneurs to include Jay Abraham, Darren Hardy and Nick Nanton.

Outside of her professional growth and business accomplishments, Megan met and married an amazing man and her favorite business partner. They reside in Atlanta, GA and delight in the joys of watching their two-year-old son Gavin grow and discover the world around him.

Keep a lookout for her future book, *People Quit People*. She would love to hear from you! Connect with her at: megan@peoplequitpeople.com with your stories, suggestions, and successes in which empowering people powered your business.

CHAPTER 8

REWARD ON INVESTMENT

BY RIAN KINNEY

I had just returned to my position as a foreclosure litigator after my mother died unexpectedly in an accident. The firm was understanding of the week I needed to mourn with family, and even had flowers and a gift basket waiting for me upon my return to the office. Three days after my one year anniversary with the firm I was called to the conference room without being given a reason.

Two people from human resources sat solemnly, and stared at me for awhile as if they didn't know what to say or how to begin so I started the conversation. "I want to thank you for the amazing opportunity to work here. In the past year I believe you have come to know how much I love and appreciate the people (and the free lattes), but I know you lost over half your litigation volume six months ago, and you can't afford to keep everyone."

Stunned, the firm manager asked, "Why do you think we are letting you go?" Trying to lighten the mood, I replied, "Well if this were an anniversary party, I imagine there would have been cake and you would have invited more people. But seriously, you've laid people off throughout the day, including my paralegal, and no one from the firm notified me that he was let go. I assume you saved me until the end of the day because you weren't sure how I might react given my mother's recent passing, but this is business, I understand it's not personal and I will be fine." She went on to explain what I already knew, that the firm should have done the layoffs around Christmas, but they were hoping to sign new clients which never materialized.

I did not panic because I believe in the Law of Attraction and I know that everything happens for a reason, in its time. So what most people might see as an overwhelming tragedy, losing my job less than a month after losing my mother, to me was a catalyst and an opportunity to begin the next chapter of my life. I actually left that conference room feeling a little excited. I didn't know what I was going to do, but whatever it was would be better than the situation I was leaving.

You see, long hours in a high-paced, high-volume, and thankless job with no opportunity for advancement, where deadlines were often missed, and mediocrity was sufficient, had taken its toll on me. I had what many considered a "good job", well-paying with benefits. But it wasn't good for me, I hated my life. I was working ten-hour days for the banks, foreclosing on people's homes without the opportunity for advancement; I had gained significant weight, used food for solace, had no energy to exercise, or to attempt a social life. Perhaps most telling of how dire my unhappiness was, was being prescribed anti-anxiety medication for ongoing chest pain. I knew the job was hurting me, but it was hard to quit a good paycheck when I had sizeable student loans and financial obligations.

Unfortunately my experience is not unique. Many people find themselves working jobs that make them miserable because, much like I did, they evaluate their lives strictly from a financial perspective. Most of us justify our choice to merely exist instead of live with thoughts like, "Yes the job sucks, but I need the money and the job security." One thing that is abundantly clear, by watching multi-million dollar firms implode and institute mass layoffs, is that there is no job security while you are working for someone else. The layoff was the push I needed, I knew there had to be something better for me than squandering my time and talent for someone else's benefit, especially in a job that left me so unfulfilled.

Launching my own business has been the adventure of a lifetime. It was scary at times, extremely challenging and yet more rewarding than anything I had ever accomplished working for someone else. I have lost forty-five pounds, I no longer have chest pains due to stress, I have cultivated an amazing network of friends, family and clients and I love my life. The ability to transition to self-employment is not limited to lawyers. In fact, a lot of what I do professionally is not lawyering at all these days.

Today, I still work with small businesses as an attorney, but more of my time is spent as a conscientious corporate consultant and transformational life coach. I help clients identify skills sets, passion and purpose in order to create the business that will accomplish their personal and professional goals, and afford them the greatest satisfaction. Sharing what I have learned on my journey of self-employment, so others can avoid common mistakes and pitfalls, has become my mission.

While I needed the push of losing a job I didn't love, you can decide that you are done trading your time, health and happiness for what someone else determines you are worth, and job security that does not exist. With the necessary information and proper planning, you can redefine what success means to you. You can be your own boss, and create a business that doesn't just offer financial returns on investment but additional rewards, such as freedom to choose your projects and clients, or determine your own schedule to create the work-life balance that leads to the happiest and healthiest you.

There are so many factors to consider and analyze when planning a business that cannot be adequately covered in this chapter. I detail how to conscientiously create the business you desire and deserve more completely in my book, Reward on Investment, I would like to share the single biggest factor to contemplate when starting your business; "The BIG Secret" that can determine your ultimate success or failure:

The question - WHY?

Why are you creating this company?

You may think this is a simple question and have a very quick and ready response. "I want to make more money, have more free time" are great answers, but the boost in income and free time is earned only after you have invested the time and resources to start and build your company. So when you're starting out and you know you will have long days and money going out before it comes back in, why you are really committed to building a business will help you maintain your focus and hold steadfast—when returning to a paycheck seems tempting.

Your answer, after you have spent time reflecting on what really matters to you, may surprise you. We all have needs, dreams and desires that go so far beyond the financial return on the investment of our time and life. We all seek rewards such as health, happiness, expressing our creativity, helping others or making a difference, for example. Let's imagine that your financial needs are going to be met by any business you create and you will have more flexibility in creating your schedule; what would you do if you knew you could not fail?

You have the ability to re-define success for yourself and conscientiously create your business using more parameters than just time and money. For instance, would it be important to you that your business is environmentally friendly? Or that your business is able to give back to the community in some way? Is it important to you to have a minority-owned business? Is it important to manufacture in America? Creating a business allows you to do more than make a living and determine your day, you get to use your profit for power make a positive impact and create a business that shares your values and of which you can be proud.

If being environmentally friendly is important to you, there is an entire business community out there committed to going green and decreasing carbon footprints. There are cross-promotional opportunities and support available to you from other like-minded entrepreneurs. You are not in this alone. If it's important for you to give back to the community, how? Will you donate products, a portion of proceeds or hire employees that need rehabilitation? Answering these questions will determine whether you start a non-profit or a separate foundation to handle donations, and there · are resources and support, especially from the recipient organizations, to assist you in setting up your donation or hiring programs and better understanding some of the tax implications and breaks.

The government has special programs for allocating contracts to minority-owned, women and veteran-owned, businesses. Very clearly identifying why you are starting your business will help you find your niche, and more than likely guide you to find a community with other like-minded small business owners that will encourage and mentor you.

If you stopped contemplating your reason for going into business at the superficial: I want more money and free time, you failed to find your passion. Successful companies have passion to innovate and provide value. You must know your passion because customers will not buy from you because you want to make money and have more free time, they buy from you because you have passion to create something they need and provide customer service that makes them feel appreciated. Why are your goods or services different or better than the competition's? How can you add more value for your customers?

Your answer to this question helps you identify your strengths and differentiate yourself – the first step in identifying your brand.

Why you are building the company also includes the why and how you would like to exit. Many people do not contemplate the end of a business at the beginning, but doing so helps in its creation. Do hope to sell or franchise it? Your answer will assist you to determine the ideal corporate entity for your business and provide a framework for how you develop your brand identity and grow your company. Franchising is a complex process and you may ultimately need to consult an attorney, but there are online resources that will provide an overview and discuss the importance of creating a strong brand name, website, logo, etc.

Once you have completed the critical task of why you want to start your business, the tools you formally plan and start a business with, are available online; organizations such as the Small Business Administration have free tools to:

1. Guide you through the process of assessing your strengths and weaknesses
2. Project a budget based on operating costs
3. Accurately calculate necessary start-up costs

Such start-up costs should include costs for an attorney, accountant or business consultant for advice and assistance after you have completed the preliminary planning. These professional costs are not as prohibitive as they once were, and in many instances, you can negotiate work on a flat-fee or per project basis to only pay for time you actually need when you are just getting started. The more questions you have answered for yourself regarding why you are building your company, your corporate values and how you plan to exit the business, and the more planning you have done will allow the professionals to better advise you and take less of their time, and your money. You will be surprised how quickly people, resources and circumstances are attracted into your life to support you in building your business when you decide to do it and are clear on why.

Understanding the law of attraction means you know your thoughts and desires create everything in your life, and it is always for your highest and best good, even if you do not understand why at the time. Sometimes life presents opportunities disguised as obstacles. I lost my job and gained a career. You are meant for far more than trading your life for dollars. If you are unhappy and unfulfilled, why? You have the power to choose differently and when you take the time to honestly ask yourself and deeply contemplate what you want, the Universe will support you.

When you choose to launch your company knowing your purpose, how you define success and why you are building a successful business, you will not just create a better life for you and your family, but at the very least your renewed health and happiness will positively impact those around you, and you may even make a bigger impact by creating jobs and a great work environment—giving back to the community and support causes that are important to you. It is my wish that sharing the Big Secret with you will put you on your path to conscientiously create the career of your dreams.

About Rian

Rian Kinney is committed to living life to the fullest; she has eaten fire, tried out for American Idol, been skydiving, is a licensed SCUBA diver and half marathoner, an avid world traveler and is currently in the process of completing her first book.

Rian began practicing law in 2009, and after learning "The Big Secret" later launched The Kinney Firm, P.A., a Florida Real Estate and Entertainment Law Firm.

Rian works as an attorney, transformational life coach and conscientious business consultant to build brands and companies that are making the world a better place. Her clients range from organic juice companies to children's authors and musicians and everything in between. She assists clients and entrepreneurs to identify their purpose and conscientiously create a company that is not just poised for success, but is also committed to positively impact the world.

Florida Entertainment Law assists clients with everything from corporate formation and securing intellectual property assets to long term legal strategy and litigation. With a focus on limiting legal risk, Rian works with clients to educate and empower them to make informed business decisions that are aligned with their purpose and values.

You can connect with Rian at:
- Legal@FLEntertainmentLaw.com
- www.twitter.com/TheKinneyFirm
- www.facebook.com/RianKinney

CHAPTER 9

MY BIG SECRET

HOW DRYING THE DISHES CHANGED MY LIFE!

BY ALAN BONNER

As I stood at the kitchen sink, drying the dishes, I knew that what I had just heard was wrong and that it was wrong on many levels.

It was a beautiful sunny autumn morning, and I had only just arrived home from kids' football. My eight-year-old son, Ben, played in a seven-a-side league, every Saturday. At the end of the game, Ben and his young team mate Ewan, stood before me, their smiling faces looking up at mine as if they were expecting a treat, chocolate or such like. Excitedly, Ewan asked if he could come back to our house to hang out and play. I checked that it was okay with Ewan's father and we were soon in the car, heading home. The boys had only been in the house for around half an hour, but they were already bored, and I could hear them putting on their shoes. As they walked past the kitchen door to head out into the garden, I heard my son Ben, say to Ewan, "I'd love it if my Dad could do that with me but he can't, he just can't, he's always working!

I stopped for a moment to question myself, did I really hear what I just heard? It was painful, a sharp stabbing pain. I looked down and in my hands was a green tea plate, which I was drying at the time. I just stared at the plate, replaying Ben's comment in my head. It was an innocuous sentence, but it hurt. My immediate reaction was to call Ben back into the house, to ask him what he meant. How could he say that? How could he be so disrespectful? After all, here we were in a wonderful big house, surrounded by spacious private gardens and lots of "material things."

I felt a tear form on my cheek, tears weren't allowed when I was growing up, it wasn't part of the culture to show any emotion in my childhood. I had come from nothing, from hand-me-down clothes and trousers that barely covered my ankles. I worked tirelessly to create a better life; I understood from an early age, that anyone could achieve greatness if they wanted it badly enough and if they put in the work, so I did. I was now a successful entrepreneur, I had started my first business in 1984 and then another and another, and somehow, despite all my failings and my setbacks, I just kept going.

I was the founder and Chief Executive of a public company which was listed on the London Stock Exchange. Building a business is tough, and running a public company is incredibly challenging. There are all kinds of outside influences; shareholders, fund managers, corporate financiers, nominated advisors, brokers, not to mention a colossus of transparency and compliance issues to endure.

I worked sixteen hours per day, and also on evenings during the weekend. I had done so for the past fifteen years in this business. The company came first, before everything, before anyone, before anything else. I thought that was the right thing to do. I believed that everything I did was for the benefit of us, our family.

As I wiped the tear from my cheek, I realised something; here was my youngest son telling his friend, that "he'd love it if his dad could do that," do what exactly? Play hide and seek? Draw a picture? Go to the park? I certainly didn't think Ben was talking about anything significant; I figured it was something simple, something ordinary.

I didn't really do "ordinary." And that's when it struck me. What am I doing? I thought. Why am I doing it? And who am I doing it for? I asked myself. I believed I was doing it for us, but if I couldn't even do ordinary things with my family, what's the point?

I'll never forget that day. It changed my life forever.

What happened next was extraordinary, for the first time in my business career, it seemed as though the company was no longer occupying most of my thoughts. I would look in the mirror in bewilderment and wonder who was looking back. I would ponder where I was and how I had gotten here. I started to marvel about where I wanted to go in life, and if I was on a path to get there. Life seemed weird!

I needed time to think, so I headed to the mountains, to Austria. The altitude of 3200 metres created a sense of peace and tranquility. It was easy to focus, to see things from a different perspective, and that's when it occurred to me; I asked myself the question; "If I wasn't in business and was home with my family most of the time, what should I do?"

I had an epiphany; that I would spend the rest of my life, helping ambitious, growth-focused people, to avoid all the mistakes that I had made. That I would take my thirty years of experience, knowledge and expertise and help people accomplish their goals, what they needed to do, why they needed to do it, and how to achieve it.

The next evening, from my Austrian apartment, I held a group phone call and told the team. In the days that followed, I made a London Stock Exchange announcement, informing the market I was going to seek my successor and retire from the board. And I did! Several months later, and immediately following completion of the company's Annual General Meeting, I stood looking up at the London sky, in astonishment. Did I just do that? Did I just retire from my own company? It was sixteen years to the day on which I had formed the business. It was surreal, a feeling of excitement and discombobulation.

In the years that followed, I read and studied everything I could get my hands on, or get access to, or events I could attend in person, or online. I wanted to understand fully, what made some people successful and others look like failures. Why some people persisted and others fell at the first hurdle. Why some people wanted riches and others settled for poverty.

I met with multi-millionaires, public figures, sports people, entrepreneurs and struggling individuals. I also engaged with parents and children from underprivileged families. I synthesized everything I had amassed. And together with all my personal experience, knowledge, and expertise, I uncovered The Big Secret. Which is that getting from where you are, to where you want to be, is actually quite simple, it's just not easy. That's it!

Put simply; you will never get to where you want to go unless you stop heading where you're currently going. Unfortunately, very few people create the position, or take the time-out that is required, to look at life as a blank sheet of paper. To map out a vision and then create a plan to fulfil that vision. Sadly, most honest, hardworking people, get to the end of their lives and realise that they never actually lived at all.

It's because most of us believe that always being busy is a good thing, but being constantly busy is not a guaranteed recipe for success. There comes a time in your life when you need to stop, take a breath and take stock of where you are. Think about how you got here and decide from this point forward, where you want to be in the future. If you don't, you'll keep on being busy until it's too late to do anything about it.

So, based on what I have learned over the decades, here is my abridged version of the first five steps to becoming wiser, wealthier and happier, as you move from stuck to significance.

Step 1: STOP!

Since we started school, we've been busy, always something to do, somewhere to go, some place to be. It's relentless, we are all too busy doing stuff, struggling, fighting, enduring, and pushing ourselves to the limit.

But here's the point; to get to your desired destination in life, you must stop what you're doing. Because it's only when you step off the roller coaster of life, and let the feeling of motion leave your body entirely, that you get a sense of what it's like to live.

So, take the time to reflect, to look forward, and to dream about what you would like the rest of your life to be. What you would like to achieve, what contribution you would like to make, and how you would like to be remembered, when you're gone.

Step 2: Dream your Vision

Creating your vision is a two-stage process. As they say in business, start with the end in mind, the same goes for planning the rest of your life.

1. Start by thinking about what it looks like when you're gone. Think about your life partner, family and friends, do they miss you? What do you want them to say about your passing? What contributions did you make to the community, etc.? Write down in as much detail as you can, what your legacy looks like and how you want to be remembered.
2. Then take a step back and look at your retirement. When you've retired from "normal life" where do you want to live, what kind of house, size, location, etc.? When you open the shades or draw back the curtains in the morning, what do you see? Do you see the mountains? The ocean? The city? What do you see? What does the kitchen look like? Do you have a garage? What vehicles do you drive? Write down in great detail what your life looks like in retirement, where you live, how you live, who you live with, what you get up to, etc.

Step 3: Segment

Now that you have a vision of what you want your life to look like, you need to break your life into measurable parts. Each segment should represent an area of your life that is most important to you. For example;

- Physical Health ~ feel, look, weight, exercise, diet, habits, disease, energy levels
- Mental ~ feelings about life, confidence, optimism, cynicism, pessimism
- Life Partner ~ married, spouse, single, partner
- Family ~ children, grandchildren
- Work ~ career, business, volunteering, job
- Legacy ~ contribution, making a difference, giving back
- Finances ~ wealth, debt, investments, savings, assets, income
- Learning ~ knowledge, reading, new skills, further education
- Social ~ networking, clubs, organisations
- Religion ~ faith, spirituality
- Character ~ compassion, honesty, integrity, courage, self-discipline
- Personal ~ adventure, fun, experiences, enjoyment

Step 4: Purpose

Next, write a purposeful statement about each segment of your life. For example, Physical Health:

I am my perfect weight, I exercise every day, usually by walking for a minimum of 3 miles. I have a healthy balanced diet, and I drink lots of water. I have high levels of energy. My body is strong and free from disease.

Continue until you have written, in as much detail as possible, a purposeful statement about each segment of your life.

Once you have written your vision and purpose, you must treasure it as if your life depends on it, why? Because it does!

Step 5: Planning

Now you need to create a plan, which will break down all of the required steps into S.M.A.R.T goals. For each life segment, start listing all the new things you'll need to start doing, what you'll need to do less of, more of, and stop doing altogether. List the people you will need help from, the resources and the time required, to come up with short-term and medium-term goals. The immediate focus will be on achieving a paradigm shift, one year from now and then five years from now.

Building your dream life is really quite simple, it's just not easy, and it's going to look like a lot of work, it is! It's painful too. But here's the thing, you will either endure the pain of self-discipline – now, or deal with the pain of regret - later, either way, there's going to be pain!

Perhaps this helps us understand why 97% of the population do not have goals, and only 1% have written goals. But please don't be put off by this and don't worry about how you're going to achieve your goals, it doesn't matter - not yet! Why? Because by the time you have completed these first five steps, you will have created an intention so powerful, that people will go out of their way to help you achieve it. As soon as you start sharing your goals (and you must), the magic will commence. People, opportunities and all sorts of things will start to appear, things that will assist you in the achievement of your goals.

So, trust in the process, it works for everyone courageous enough to pursue it, and it will work for you too.

About Alan

Alan Bonner is recognised as one of the UK's leading authorities on entrepreneurship. With an unshakable belief that anyone can achieve greatness, Alan is a serial entrepreneur who has built many multi-million turnover businesses.

A Best-Selling Author and Quilly® Award Winner, Professional Speaker and Expy® Award Winner, Alan Bonner's philosophies have been featured in *Forbes* magazine. Alan has been inducted into the National Academy of Best Selling Authors® and the National Association of Experts, Writers, and Speakers™. Alan has appeared on The Brian Tracy Show, and has been seen on NBC, ABC, CBS, and FOX affiliates around the country. In parallel to his business success, Alan Bonner is also a highly-accomplished racing driver, with over 25 years of motorsport under his belt.

Since retiring from his last business, which joined the London Stock Exchange in 2007, Alan dedicates his time to transforming the lives of ambitious, growth-oriented business owners, professionals and entrepreneurs. By sharing his 30 years of knowledge, experience and expertise, Alan focuses on "making the simple - easy," using his step-by-step success system, which moves people from stuck to significance. In the process, his clients discover how to live life fully, by becoming wiser, wealthier and happier.

Alan was also a producer on *Maximum Achievement*, the Brian Tracy story, and *The Soul Of Success*, the Jack Canfield story.

You can find out more and connect with Alan at:
- www.AlanBonner.com

CHAPTER 10

HARMONIOUS SOUNDS OF SUCCESS

A STORY OF PEACE THROUGH MUSIC

BY DUDLEY EVENSON

Our story of following and manifesting our dreams is unique, but then so is everyone's story. We each are born with our own set of gifts and talents to which we add our energy, dedication and focus. I believe with all my heart that success in life is an option for everyone, no matter where they begin. The important thing is to look deeply at what lights you up and then cultivate that with all your passion.

My husband Dean and I make music, 80 albums worth so far, garnering worldwide distribution and many awards. There is much more music stirring within us. Dean plays the flute and was trained as a professional recording engineer. He also holds a Master's Degree in Molecular Biology. I have my own musical areas of expertise involving harp, vocal toning and percussion. Making music came naturally to us and we leaned in, but the secret to our success isn't about our musical talent.

We were activists for peace throughout the '60s and were finding our own voice throughout the amazing experiences we had – using cutting edge technology to videotape the pivotal places and people of the day. Especially enlightening was being involved with the struggles of America's indigenous peoples. We were learning a lot, but it came with its risks, and in many cases we gave up security and certainty to follow our dreams. I'd say this was especially true when we lived out of our bus in the '70s, during what we called our "decade of intentional poverty." We were trading comfort for principle, but we were happy to do it.

With video camera in hand, we set out to seek answers for our probing question of how to live a happy and healthy life in harmony with nature itself. We really got clear about who we are and why we were born. We discovered not just what we were against, but what we stood FOR. This was a critical bit of learning that would influence everything that was to come. As we challenged ourselves to learn and evolve, a path was opening before us, and that path was illuminating a powerful way to spread our values through music.

We both were profoundly impacted by what we were exposed to during the transformative years of the '60s and '70s, especially so with the Native American ideology that the Earth is a living being. This was revolutionary and inspiring to us! As a consequence, our music has been heavily influenced by, and infused with the sounds and rhythms of nature. It's no small wonder our record label was aptly named Soundings of the Planet, and *Peace Through Music* became our motto.

We knew we had a mission, a purpose and even a vehicle to carry us forward. We also received immediate validation we were on the right track. We initially sold our music at swap meets and later at craft fairs and wellness conferences. Massage therapists were really the first group of people to discover our albums, and soon people used them for yoga, meditation and quiet time. Testimonials came in from our listeners who told us how the music helped them let go of stress or even deal with chronic pain or disease.

By selling directly to the public, we got immediate feedback that our peaceful music with natural sounds helped people become more relaxed and often had a healing effect. A children's cancer ward used our tapes to soothe anxious patients. Mothers in childbirth used our music as well as stressed out corporate business people who desperately needed to calm down.

Our music was benefitting people in many exciting ways. One day we received a call from Grammy award-winning country singer, Naomi Judd, who used our music to help deal with her Hepatitis. She believed in the music's benefits so strongly that she would buy our tapes to give out to people she met in her travels.

Because our music elicited such positive feedback related to relaxation and healing, we decided to research exactly what was going on and how it was working. We discovered that music, by its nature, is a link between the external and internal worlds, a bridge to the spirit and doorway to soul. We learned that sound affects the vibratory rate of every part of the body and has a direct impact on the mental processes, muscles, nervous system, digestive system and circulatory system.

Tension in the mind translates itself into tension in the body and can cause a state of dis-ease in the body's organs and systems. The American Institute for Preventative Medicine cites stress as a key role player and contributing factor in both heart disease and cancer, two of the leading causes of death in the United States. Best-selling author and physician, Dr. Andrew Weil, concurs saying, "I am convinced that stress is the primary cause or aggravating cause of the majority of illness."

We wanted to understand why our music and healing went so well together. We found that in addition to the pleasant environment the music provides, there are many reasons why music can actually support the healing process. In his landmark book, *The Mozart Effect*, Don Campbell states that, "by listening to music with longer, slower sounds, one can usually deepen and slow the breath, allowing the mind to calm down. As with breathing rates, a lower heartbeat creates less physical tension and stress, calms the mind, and helps the body heal itself. Music is a natural pacemaker."

How exactly how does music support health and wellbeing? We knew that healing music is much more than just slow music with nature sounds. In case you're interested, here are some reasons we found for how it works to alleviate stress:

- Slow rhythms entrain bodily systems (heartbeat, pulse, digestive system, respiratory, muscles) to a more natural rhythm
- Natural sounds (if present) give a sense of peace
- Tones are nurturing, clear, warm and gentle
- Pace is slow but with a sense of joy and beauty
- Music doesn't have hooks and repeated refrains that engage the mind

- Feeling is more like nature, flowing
- Sub-audio frequencies (if present) entrain brainwaves to alpha or theta state
- Intention of both the musician and listener are important

It was becoming clear to us that a relaxed body and sense of inner calm are beneficial to restoring health and maintaining balance in the face of stress and disease. Often, the mind needs an extra tool to assist it in letting go of disturbing or repetitive thoughts that might be holding us back from reaching our highest potential. Music has the ability to give the mind another focus and thus it helps lower stress levels, which in turn helps strengthen the immune system.

We realized that healing is about re-aligning the body with its own innate blueprint and returning to a dynamic state of balance from a temporary state of imbalance. Of the many tools that help us deal with stress, music can complement them all. Mind-body modalities such as yoga, meditation, affirmations, visualization, vocal toning, mantra, chanting, and guided imagery can all be enhanced by the presence of relevant music.

When we take hold of our thoughts and use music and affirmations regularly, success is bound to occur in our lives. By visualizing and feeling the reality of our spoken word affirmations, we enter into a cooperative contract with the universe to make use of these powerful tools to manifest our highest dreams.

In our case, we began by following our hearts, by exposing ourselves to the vast diversity of knowledge and human experience the world has to offer. We grew in clarity about who we are, and what we stand for, and then we followed through with our natural talents in alignment with a singular mission – Peace Through Music – world peace, inner peace, personal peace, physical peace.

Today, we're still leaning in to this journey! I'm using so much of what we've learned in my life-coaching business. We both apply the best of what we now know to make even more music and videos to send positive ripples of peace around the world. When I said that our musical success wasn't about our musical talents, I meant it. It was really about our ability to be clear, consciously evolve, and then to lean in.

Some simple principles that have guided us:

- Know who you are and what your values are.
- Dream big dreams, not just for yourself, but in service to others.
- Have the faith and courage to take risks and follow your dreams.
- Be perseverant and do the daily work to make it happen.
- What you focus on expands. Apply single-mindedness.
- Be creative and change direction when necessary.
- Get help. Cooperate. Collaborate. Share.
- Stay positive and don't let adversity stop you.
- Deal with stress by learning to control your mind.
- When you fall down, pick yourself back up and keep going.
- Music, meditation and affirmations are tools that can help.
- Cultivate a spiritual practice that includes gratitude.

It won't always be easy, it won't always be simple, but the right mental and acoustic soundtrack can make all the difference in the world! We wish you the best in your process and hope our paths will cross along the way. May you find Peace through Music, however that works for you.

About Dudley

Dudley Evenson is a multi-media producer, writer and life coach who has been living her dreams for five decades and loves to teach others how to live theirs. She also plays harp with her husband, Dean Evenson, whom she met in 1968. They have been spiritual, musical and business partners ever since.

During the 1970s, Dudley and Dean traveled with their young family in a half-sized, converted school bus documenting the new consciousness that was emerging. Their use of the newly-released portable video camera placed them as pioneers of a technological revolution that continues to this day. It was the first time that such high-tech video media was available to everyday people, a concept taken for granted now with smart phones, but brand new and transformative then.

At the end of the decade, after making hundreds of hours of videos with no way to distribute them, she and her flautist husband, Dean, side-stepped back into audio and co-founded their music label, Soundings of the Planet. Their entrepreneurial spirit and musical talents propelled them as pioneers into the field of sound healing. Their award-winning music is used in far ranging settings from hospitals and yoga centers to prisons, schools and workplaces to support people's healing and life process.

Over the course of many decades, they traveled to gatherings of new thought leaders and sold their music or presented workshops on meditation and sound healing. By 2017, the Evensons had produced over 80 albums and videos and their music had been enjoyed by millions around the world.

Dudley has created a series of guided affirmations recordings and popular online courses. Her teachings focus on the self-healing wisdom that she and Dean have discovered during their spiritual quest over almost half a century.

Her blog, videos and articles cover a range of topics including healing with music, meditation, relationships, affirmations, and manifesting success. Dudley also writes guidebooks on 'healthy living' themes such as how to meditate with music, healing relationships, etc.

These days, after years of traveling to conferences and workshops, Dudley and Dean are content staying home in their cottage by a wild river in a forested valley of the Cascade Mountains. Dean walks to the barn studio in the morning for his daily exercise routine and to work on his music and media. Dudley does her thing in the house reaching out to the world, coaching and keeping Soundings going. Later they may meet in the garden, or take a hike across the field to the river. Every night is date night. Dinner and a movie followed by music. That's what happens when you marry your soul mate.

Sometimes Dudley and Dean go into town to work in their main Soundings studio. Next to the studio are three houses the Evensons purchased back during boom times and still own. They form a semi-intentional community where friends, musicians, healers, gardeners, builders, entrepreneurs, and filmmakers live. The dream keeps manifesting as the peaceful music continues to reach out around the world.

Connect with Dudley Evenson: −−

(I) Soundings Music & Blog:
- www.soundings.com
- 800/93 PEACE

(II) Social Media:
- www.facebook.com/soundingsoftheplanet
- www.youtube.com/soundingsoftheplanet
- www.facebook.com/dudleyevenson
- www.twitter.com/dudleyevenson
- www.instagram.com/dudleyevenson

CHAPTER 11

THE 7-KEY SYSTEM FOR SELF-EMPOWERMENT AND LIFE SUCCESS

BY JOSE M. BALTAZAR, Ph.D.

- Do you have any goals that seem to elude you?
- Do you have greater desires and wonder if you will achieve them?
- Do you have any big dreams to accomplish and they seem too far away?
- Do you consider yourself successful but desire to achieve greater successes?
- Are there areas in your life that you want to improve or wish they were better?
- Would you like to be totally certain that you will accomplish all your dreams?
- Would you like to get to your dreams in good health?
- Would you like to achieve your goals much faster and easier?

Anyone who answers "yes" to any of these questions would benefit greatly by changing their life-style to live it within my 7-Key System. I have been using this system of personal growth and self-improvement for over 20 years. I have taught my model to a diverse population. I have used it with people of all ages, creeds, color, professions, and socio-economic status. My system has proven effective for the vast majority of individuals. I have taught my system to teachers and parents so they can use it on themselves and others and they also report effective results. I have conducted four studies, two with a control-group in them. These studies demonstrate my system to be effective. But what excites me the most is the hundreds of testimonials I have collected through the years. I would like to share my journey with you by sharing some of the stories that have inspired me to continue developing myself as a person and professional. Through all the experiences like the ones I share with you here, *I have developed a personal mission to help people accomplish their goals and desires easier and faster and with the least stress possible while providing them health and wellness benefits.* I accomplish this mission through my **7-Key System for Self-Empowerment and Life Success.**

Mary was a young failing college student who was sent to me with a diagnosis of learning disabilities longer than a weekly grocery list. She started crying as soon as she came into my office. She had just been told by a psychologist to forget about becoming a teacher and to settle for a shorter and easier career choice. I enrolled Mary in my Student Success Course and worked with her a few times individually. In less than a year, she raised her grade point average to 3.5 and became the president of the Honors Society.

The last time I saw Mary, she was already working as an Elementary School Teacher, and was considering a job as a trainer at an aero-space company. Below is a portion of a letter of appreciation she wrote to me:

"I learned a lot about accelerated learning with Mr. Baltazar, and I started practicing the techniques he taught me. I used to be a "C" or "D" student and now my grades have improved to "A" and "B". Mr. Baltazar taught me some very helpful techniques that started working for me right away, so that I decided to enroll in his Accelerated Learning Study Skills class. I have learned many more techniques that help me emotionally as well as academically. I am very thankful to Mr. Baltazar for all the help he has given me."

Pat was working at a community college as a paraprofessional in the social work and counseling fields. She was in her late 30's and had always dreamed of becoming a Counselor for the same institution. When I met Pat she shared her dream with me but would always end stating that it was too late, she was not smart enough, it would take forever to get a counselor position even if she got her master's degree, etc. I invited Pat to work with me and after a few sessions she made the decision to enroll in a counseling master's program, completed it with honors, got the counseling position she wanted, has received the Faculty Achievement Award, and is running one of the counseling centers at the same institution. Pat also teaches Student Success courses and has become one of my best friends and a promoter of my approach for coaching people to greater success, achievement, and fulfillment.

For over 44 years I have been working with individuals, most of them college and university students, and professionals wanting to overcome obstacles that seem to hold them back from moving on to the next step in achieving worthwhile goals and dreams. However, for the last 26 years, I have experienced the most joy and satisfaction in my career because of a discovery I made back in 1991. After delving into traditional training and teaching pedagogy and approaches, and noticing that regardless of how much money in financial aid the government provided, the graduation rates in colleges and universities, except elite ones, oscillated between 20% and 25%, while the High School drop-out rate was also a staggering 50%; I decided to look into alternative and non-traditional approaches to teaching and learning. In 1991, while attempting to help a bright student (A- grade average) who had been kicked out of the Nursing Program at my institution, and who's liver had actually ripped open due to the stress and demands of the program; I ran into a methodology of learning called *Accelerated Learning.*

In my research, I saw the reference to a book titled *Super-Learning.* This book changed my life and the life of this student. I read it from beginning to end over a weekend and extracted one of the techniques the authors shared. I taught it to my student and asked her to practice it for two weeks. She came back after two weeks and she looked happy, healthy, and excited. She had her little girl with her who was listening to music on her walk-man cassette player (...remember those?). She gave me a hug and thanked me. She had been accepted back into the nursing program, and was looking forward to resume her studies. Then she asked me a question: What do you think my daughter is listening to? What? I asked. She told me her daughter had been listening to the music I had asked her to use as part of the technique I had taught her. She stated that her daughter was diagnosed with attention deficit disorder (ADD) and that her daughter's teacher had communicated to her that lately she had been so focused on her classes, and was getting good grades. Since then, I have seen other "miracles" in performance improvement in other people I've coached that are too many to describe. I knew I had run into something special and powerful to help people become better learners and achievers.

I started researching the field of Accelerated Learning more in depth. I bought a few books and training manuals, and started attending conferences and trainings in the field. I've had many more significant experiences in helping people that have shaped me and have contributed to the development of my model. What I had learned so far through Accelerated Learning was that in addition to be able to move forward in life faster and easier, people were also obtaining health and wellness benefits. My clients would frequently share with me that besides being able to overcome obstacles in their life's progress, they were experiencing health benefits like elimination of low back pains, ceasing of headaches, being able to sleep much better, regulation of high blood pressure, regulation of blood sugar levels, etc. My most recent experience is becoming familiar with the field of *Mind-Body Medicine* and obtaining my Ph.D. in this science. This experience taught me why my clients and students were experiencing health benefits in addition to getting their goals realized. Getting my Ph.D. in *Mind-Body Medicine* has cemented my belief in the power of the human being to live a happier, more prosperous, and more achieving life while remaining healthy, and without having to strive so hard, and without experiencing so much unhealthy stress in their lives. I refer to my approach as *"Relaxed and Accelerated Success."*

THE 7-KEY SYSTEM MODEL

My 7-Key System for Self-Empowerment and Life Success has at its core the science of relaxation and meditation. I practiced relaxation and meditation since early in my life but I was not aware of the science behind it. I became familiar with the Law of Attraction before I became familiar with the science that makes it work. You've probably seen the movie and have heard of all the motivating phrases that imply the power behind The Law of Attraction. Here are some phrases we have been hearing for a long time:

- "Whatever your mind can conceive and believe, you can achieve." ~ Napoleon Hill
- "The ability of the individual to think is his ability to act on the Universal and bring it into manifestation." ~ Charles F. Hannel

- "Success is determined not so much by the size of one's brain as it is by the size of one's thinking." ~ David J. Schwartz
- "Whether you think you can or think you can't, you are right." ~ Henry Ford
- "Whatever you ask for in prayer believe that you will receive it and it shall be yours." ~ The Bible

The Law of Attraction movie showed us that to get what we want, we need to visualize it vividly in our mind and feel the feelings we would experience as if we already had that which we want.

All these philosophical ways of thinking are right and true. A critical factor however has been left out when the philosophies are taught to other people. It is interesting to me that even though I had been working at improving my own life for many years, until I ran into Accelerated Learning, no one had placed emphases on the science of relaxation and meditation as a way of speeding up change. The science behind Mind-Body Medicine explains, without making it its main purpose, why the Law of Attraction Works. Empowered and inspired by the results of my own studies, and hundreds of documented testimonials, I have developed my holistic and integrated personal change model. Below is a description of my model.

THE 7-KEY SYSTEM FOR SELF-EMPOWERMENT AND LIFE SUCCESS

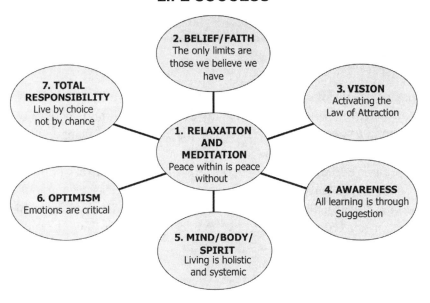

Key 1. Relaxation and Meditation

The brain is the master organ that drives behavior. In order to reprogram it for more productive behaviors it must be at the highest level of receptiveness possible. The more receptive the brain is, the easier it is for it to develop new or improve positive behaviors. Because all the other components of my model require changes in behavior you can see why this component is so critical. Through a menu of mind-body techniques such as Imagery, Autogenics, Self-hypnosis, Neuro-linguistics, the Relaxation Response, Mindfulness, Transcendental Meditation, Brain-wave Management, Sub-Conscious Learning, and others, personal change occurs much faster and easier. This menu of mind-body medicine approaches makes my model powerful and effective.

Key 2. Belief

Changing and improving beliefs is one of the first lessons of most motivators and teachers of success. Everyone agrees in the principle of believing in one-self and in the dream or goal we desire. Everyone, no matter how successful they are, can benefit from strengthening their belief in themselves and in their potential to achieve what they desire. Most recommendations and approaches to improve beliefs depend on cognitive processes. Through relaxation and meditation exercises that target improvement in self-belief, change becomes non-cognitive and penetrates deeper into the subconscious to effectuate change faster and without effort.

Key 3. Vision

Everyone has visions of what they want and desire to obtain. Some visions are unclear; others are pursued with doubt even though people really want them. Others have very clear visions of what they want and yet are unable to obtain it. What is the difference between those who realize their dreams and desires and those who struggle to or never obtain them? The answer: Consistency of positive emotion such as excitement and optimism toward their vision. Relaxation and meditation are vehicles to sustain relaxed and calmed excitement and action towards realizing dreams and desires.

Key 4. Awareness

One of the essential factors of success is attention and concentration of effort. This is also referred as focus. Interestingly enough, this skill and behavior is naturally developed by the practice of relaxation and meditation techniques.

Key 5. Mind-Body-Spirit

The mind, the body, and the spirit of a human being are one. This is a holistic principle of systems. If any one of the components is not properly taken care of, the health and performance of the system suffers and slows down significantly or deteriorates at a faster rate. Meditation and relaxation processes integrate the mind, body, and spirit of the person and develop motivation to take good care of each component to maintain high levels of energy and productivity.

Key 6. Optimism

Optimism is an attitude and a skill. Naturally optimistic people tend to be more successful than the average person. It helps anyone to learn to be more optimistic by using mental models and procedures that transform a person into a more optimistic one. Dr. Martin E.P. Seligman of the University of Pennsylvania teaches methods to learn to be more optimistic in his book, *Learned Optimism: How to Change Your Mind and Your Life*. Learning this approaches supported by relaxation and meditation makes the learning and change process much easier and faster.

Key 7. Total Responsibility

Taking total responsibility for the choices we make without excuses and without blaming anyone when things don't go our way is a major change for most people. When things don't turn out the way we expected, the tendency is to blame someone else or look for causes outside of our control. This way we feel excused for things not going our way. By living life with total responsibility focuses energy upon the individual and empowers him/her with flexibility to make new and better choices. Once again, relaxation and meditation in my model facilitate the needed change in thinking and behavior to live life with total responsibility.

There you have it. These are the seven keys for Self-empowerment and Life Success. I have been coaching clients individually and in group sessions and class settings, to run their lives according to this model for over 25 years. I am encouraged by the positive feedback I continue to receive, and by the results of studies I have recently conducted.

Intending the best for you and your loved ones always.

About Dr. Baltazar

Jose M. Baltazar, Ph.D. is the president and owner of El Paso OASIS, Center for Accelerated Learning and Holistic Health in El Paso, Texas. Dr. Baltazar's passion is to help people achieve their dreams and desires while maintaining a healthy mind, body, and spirit. He has developed "The 7-Key System for Self-empowerment and Life Success." He uses this model in his coaching practice to assist clients achieve desired goals and dreams. Dr. Baltazar is a Life Coach and Trainer, and provides training to instructors in schools on how to integrate Accelerated Learning and Mind-Body skills into their classes to improve student motivation and performance in school. He also conducts training programs and workshops for organizations and small businesses in Holistic Stress Management, Holistic Health and Nutrition, Holistic Self-Healing, and Anger Management based on *Mind-Body Medicine*.

Jose holds a doctorate degree in Mind-Body Medicine, and graduate and undergraduate degrees in Human and Organizational Development, Business Administration, and Computer Science. He has worked in higher education for over 44 years, and is an award-winning Administrator, Counselor, Instructor, and Trainer. He has extensive experience developing curriculum for courses in Computer Science, Human Motivation and Success, Accelerated Learning, Mind-Body Medicine, and Anger Management. Jose also holds certifications in *Mind-Body Medicine*, Neuro-Linguistic Programming, Accelerated Learning, Brain-Based Learning, and Choice/Reality Therapy. He is the author of three books in successful living, student success and learning skills: *Building Blocks: College Success Skills, The Accelerated Learning Companion for College Students*, and *A Course in Anger Transformation*. He is a co-author in the Best Seller series *Wakeup … Live the Life You Love*.

Dr. Jose M. Baltazar can be contacted at:
- El Paso OASIS: Center for Accelerated Learning and Holistic Health
  10600 Montwood Dr., Ste. 114, El Paso, Texas 79936
- ElPasoOASIS@yahoo.com
- Tel: 915-694-6109
- www.ElPasoOasis.com

CHAPTER 12

ONE BIG SECRET TO SUCCESS: EXCUSE YOUR EXCUSES

BY DR. KATHLEEN ROCHE

It is so easy to blame or find fault with others because it allows us to not be held accountable for our actions, choices or results.

One of the things I did best while growing up was to blame everyone for any lack or problem in my life. I refused to accept my responsibility in the things that were occurring along the way. It was when I woke up to the way I was thinking and how I was responding and reacting, that I finally saw the light at the end of the tunnel. I had been in a place where I now see most people who are struggling with their life, their success and their lack of happiness.

TAKING RESPONSIBILITY FOR YOUR OWN SUCCESS

I always knew I wanted more from life but I was unwilling to step out of my comfort zone and take chances. I did not have enough belief in myself and was looking for others to fulfill my life and create my happiness. I wanted someone to do it for me. I wanted someone to go the extra mile, and do what I was unwilling to do myself. Like most people I've talked to there is a common theme that everyone has had it better or easier. The excuses are endless.

I started asking myself why are some individuals able to succeed and others are not. Even with the same education, upbringing and opportunities? It was when I began searching for the answers that I realized they were there all along, I was just not "seeing" them.

I began reading and studying success principles and successful people. It surprised me that they too had overcome fears, doubts, and failures in their life. They made many of the same excuses that I made and even blamed others for their lack of happiness or success. It was when they took charge of their life and decided to be responsible for it that things changed for them.

ASK FOR HELP

Another thing that was holding me back was my inability to seek help from others. I had the attitude that I could do it all myself and thought I knew more than I did–big mistake for success. Success requires the ability to ask for help and to follow the given advice. I thought I would be considered weak or unintelligent if I asked for help. In reality, I just did not have the courage to ask for help. I often wonder how as youth or even adults we acquire these thought processes. It is growth to get over these mindsets and take accountability for your thoughts and actions. When we can allow others into our life and allow them to be a blessing and an asset, it becomes a blessing and asset for both of us. To receive help, money, advice, guidance, and even criticism, is growth. What we do with the tools of growth will determine our outcomes and success; however, we define the word success.

When I stopped blaming others, quit using the same worn out excuses, that is when my business flourished. I grew and so did my life happiness, my monetary success and the ability to affect others with jobs, life skills, attitude changes, belief in themselves and their own successes. So I challenge you to **Excuse Your Excuses**.

FINDING SUCCESS AS A CHIROPRACTOR

In fact, the majority of people that I meet, have this misconception of chiropractic healthcare. They believe they know more about chiropractic than the doctors themselves. They have never been to a chiropractor or even spoken to a chiropractor. They just assume that they know what that healing art is all about! They make excuses for not going and believe what others have told them, even others who have not ever been to a chiropractor. Chiropractors, just like any profession, are only as good as their education, both in school and out of school. This was one reason I joined a national franchise so that I would be up-to-date on all of the latest and greatest ways to treat patients while creating a WOW experience.

When I first started in practice, I was just like most people and most chiropractors; I thought I could do everything myself but guess what? That only left me struggling and full of frustration. I thought I could not afford to seek or get help or advice or hire anyone to coach or guide me. Boy, was I wrong! That was just what I needed, but I was living in a negative, excuse-filled lifestyle which only lead to less success and of course, more excuses! So I did what I'm asking you to do and that is to step out of your comfort zone and see what chiropractic is all about. Now you are probably asking yourself what to look for in a chiropractor or a chiropractic office? Well, I am here to help you make that decision. I am here to help your mind, body and spirit. In addition to my successful chiropractic office, I wrote a book to help you achieve success your way, which you can find in one of my books, *Realize Your Potential (Ten Secrets to Success Revealed)*.

WHAT IS CHIROPRACTIC ANYWAY?

Chiropractic is a healing art which has been around for over 100 years. Chiropractic means, "practice by hand." It is a non-invasive method for treating your spine, its muscular attachments and freeing up the nerves in the area of pain or irritation. Chiropractic doctors use a variety of methods to treat patients. This decision is based upon an examination, x-rays, range of motion studies, a complete history and general observation and palpation of their patient presenting for care. For example, if a person has low back pain, in addition to looking at the back and its muscular state, we might also look at their feet and their arches, or their knees to determine if they bow in or out or if they are a contributing factor in the 'low back' complaints. We ask about the patient's lifestyle and activity levels to determine if that is a contributing factor too. If it is, we can give suggestions on how to modify the activity.

For example, patients with headaches or neck pain, we can recommend a pillow or give suggestions on how to sleep. We can make referrals to medical or orthopedic doctors for co-treatment or co-management of the patient. If we determine we need additional testing, we can send for CT-scans or MRI's. *The job of the chiropractor is to eliminate pain and get a "joint" or bone in the spine "unstuck" or moving again.* This movement will eliminate inflammation and create less pain. The elimination of the stuck joint will allow the body to begin its healing process.

The second part of what some, but not all, chiropractors do is to create rehab therapy plans, which incorporate exercises and strengthening programs to hold the adjusted, corrected joint in its proper place. When the joints/bones/vertebrae are in their proper place, the body can work the way it was intended, as God made us. It allows the nerves in the injured or damaged area to heal and work properly also. Each nerve can be traced to various muscles and organs in the body. The spinal cord is "housed" in the spinal column. Nerves branch out between the spinal bones and are distributed to organs and muscles. Chiropractors move the bones. The chiropractic movement of these stuck bones is called an adjustment. When we were born we were born with three curves in our spine.

After trauma, repetitive use, sports, or just general living, those curves can become decreased or flattened and this sets the body up with degeneration in those areas. This leads to pain and inflammation. If the curve through chiropractic can be restored (depending on the amount of degeneration or damage to the area), then this eliminates the pain, the inflamed nerve, the swelling and the restriction on the range of motion to that area or joint. It slows the degeneration because the body is working correctly and the increased or normal curve allows the discs between each bone to do its proper job. The job of the disc is to be a cushion for the bone and allow enough space for the nerve to exit freely from the spinal column and innervate its organ or muscle. Chiropractic treatments can be done by hand, with special instruments and even specialty tables.

THE RISK OF CHIROPRACTIC CARE IS VERY MINIMAL.

If you select a knowledgeable doctor who takes the time to do a complete examination, complete x-rays, complete history and testing, the risk is even smaller.

How to pick the best Chiropractor for your chiropractic healthcare and wellness?

I have listed the top ten reasons why patients seek us out, refer their friends, families, children and co-workers, get excellent results and stay for wellness. Are you ready to try something for pain elimination, increased mobility, better overall health without drugs and their dangerous side effects? Are you ready to make your own decision and healthcare choices? Are you ready to be pro-active and stop the pain before it gets worse or causes more problems? If so, you are an ideal candidate for chiropractic care.

Top 10 things to look for in selecting a chiropractic office:

1. Educated team members and doctors. (An office where weekly training is performed and where weekly webinars are held for all team members so everyone is a team player in your care.) An office where we listen to YOU.

2. Patient Fulfillment is Top Priority. It is not about the doctor or the team member but it is about You, the patient, and remembering that we work for you.

3. Patients are Family. Select an office where you are treated like family. An office that respects you and your healthcare concerns and needs.

4. An office which does a report of its findings. Those based upon complete examinations, computerized ranges of motion and any necessary x-rays. (X-rays can determine the integrity of your spine such as degeneration, abdominal or calcified aortas, osteoporosis or osteopenia, and will determine if any other tests or procedures are needed before ANY care is given.)

5. An office which uses treatment plans. Those plans are based upon your situation and circumstance, not cookie-cutter care. Such an office will determine your benefits for care and will help you through that process. An office which remains open and honest about the cost of care and what, if any, you will need to pay.

6. An office that celebrates the holidays and the seasons. Life is meant to be celebrated and an office which can laugh at itself (like wearing funny outfits) or getting a pie in the face for charity. It lets you know that office is full of people who are happy, and happy people make great care providers.

7. An office that is involved in their community and who gives back by donating time and money through promotions, events and community involvement.

8. Confidence of the team members and the doctors and an office which holds each other accountable. An office where everyone takes pride in giving service to others. An office of integrity, enthusiasm and positive energy of the office from your initial paperwork and examination throughout your course of care. Look for a positive and upbeat environment and a place where people want to work and are happy in their positions.

9. An office that performs progress examinations. An office which monitors and watches your progress and changes your treatment as you go or as you need. An office that evaluates what is or is not working and changes accordingly, or sends you for a referral to another specialist.

10. An office that Gets Results! An office that has testimonials and gets the job done. An office which offers Wellness plans so you can stay pain free, active and continue with your weekend warrior activities.

In Summary:

Don't let excuses slow you down. Don't blame others; take responsibility for your life, your health and your decisions. So excuse your excuses and start down the path to success and what that means in your life, personally, professionally and physically. It is important that all of these remain healthy in order for you to achieve your greatest potential for success. When one is not well the others suffer too. Good luck on your journey to success after reading this book (or my previously mentioned book), and to healthy living using chiropractic care.

About Dr. Roche

Dr. Kathleen Roche treats her patient's mind, body and spirit through chiropractic care, rehab therapy, and supplements. In addition to this, she lectures and enriches her community through teaching success tips and skills for goal achievement and life fulfillment. Dr. Roche began her chiropractic career in 1999 when she was mentored by a retiring chiropractor whose business she later purchased.

Dr. Roche treats patients like family and respects their healthcare choices and ideas. Dr. Roche attributes her success in her practice to thoroughly listening and responding to the needs and care of her patients. She has always owned her own chiropractic business and she currently successfully owns and operates a chiropractic franchise. The systems used in the franchise allowed her to grow exponentially in terms of treatment and chiropractic education. Dr. Roche also employs the same philosophies when teaching other doctors about what it takes to run a successful business and subsequently watches them grow and develop into incredible doctors, business owners, and mentors for future doctors. Dr. Roche has developed and implemented practices that work in terms of business growth and chiropractic care. Due to her hard work, doctors that are privileged to work with her are more successful, enlightened, and dedicated than they were at the start of their careers. Dr. Roche takes pride in introducing both chiropractic and success principles to others and giving back to her community.

Dr. Roche graduated from Webster University with a Bachelor's Degree in Marketing. She graduated from Logan College of Chiropractic in the top ten percent of her class. She was listed in the *Who's Who* of College students while at Logan College. Dr. Roche was on the Dean's list 8 out of 10 semesters, all while raising her kids, husband and dog! Dr. Roche was lead to HealthSource Chiropractic which is a national chiropractic franchise system. It was the mastermind experience used by HealthSource Chiropractic which introduced her to what it takes to become success orientated and to realize her potential. The selection into the mastermind gave Dr. Roche the confidence to move forward in life, challenged her thinking, and made her step out of her comfort zone. As a result she wrote her first book, *Realize Your Potential (Ten Secrets to Success Revealed).*

Dr. Roche was selected as one of the America's Premier Experts and is co-authoring a book with Jack Canfield, best known for his *Chicken Soup for the Soul* series. She has won franchise of the month twice since entering the HealthSource Chiropractic family. Dr. Roche has shared her success secrets and chiropractic knowledge at Lindenwood University in Belleville, Illinois, School District 90 in O'Fallon, Illinois, the Chamber of Commerce speaker series, personal care giver's training, nurse appreciation week, local BNI's and other small business series.

You can contact Dr. Kathleen Roche by email at:
- krochedc@gmail.com
- www.drkathleenroche.com
- Facebook at: Healthsource Swansea

CHAPTER 13

CAN FILM AND TELEVISION POSITIVELY EFFECT SOCIAL CHANGE?

BY HILARY PRYOR

I *know* it does. While we are all familiar with the blockbuster movies, the viral YouTube hits, and the thought–provoking theatrical documentaries that shape common culture, this is the story of my own personal experience as a filmmaker and my efforts to produce media that is an agent for positive change.

IN THE BEGINNING

I didn't exactly plan a career in film and television – but here's how it started. About thirty years ago I was the mother of five young children – a former social worker with extensive background in theatre. And I was concerned about the increasing influence of television on the lives of young children.

As a social worker, I had seen so many stressed homes where the TV doubled as a baby sitter. I had no problem in this *per se* – heavens, with five young kids I turned to TV myself! But not all day and every day. And I made choices about what my children were able to watch. I knew that for many children in the UK and North America, TV was a constant companion regardless of what was being shown. So, I decided to try to get involved and help produce content that would engage, stimulate and motivate kids to think for themselves and help them reach out to explore and enjoy this wonderful world of ours.

It began small. I wrote up a grant application and received a grant – a small grant – from Canada Council Explorations to work with children to produce programming with them on the topics of their choosing. At that time, I lived in a rural area – some distance from a major center and I think – in part – this was one secret of later success. I got together a group of youngsters aged between 12 and 15. And we began to discuss a variety of topics of their choice, and create shows based around them. Their choice of topics surprised me. Human rights, education, advertising, divorce, living with disabilities, immigration, justice. . . even death.

Initially, we produced shows at the local community cable station but there were many limitations. So I formed a non-profit society – ETC – Educating Toward Change – and raised money from foundations to buy equipment. I learned to operate the cameras alongside the kids. The editing suite was set up in my basement. Soon, we were putting out a weekly magazine show on local community cable. I started another group with much younger kids – tapping in to their imaginations, and we produced shows for a pre-school audience.

I began to get specific grants to produce "specials" with the older kids on topics such as drugs and alcohol, the downside of smoking, the UN Declaration of the Rights of the Child, an orientation video for kids going into hospital and many others. Each show addressed the topics in different ways – some were magazine style, some documentary, and some drama and sketch comedy. Some of the resulting films were now broadcast on Canadian educational networks. They began to win international awards. And then in 1987, I was invited to the Banff International Television Festival to appear on a panel about children's television and talk about my work. There I was introduced to the "business" of Television.

Because I had started out "in the boonies," I had learnt to do all aspects of the process myself. Now I was thrust into the heart of the television industry but, arriving with a string of awards and broadcast credits already to my name, I was   accepted as a professional filmmaker – no questions asked!

I fully believe if I had received that original grant while living in a big city, I'd most likely have been swallowed up by well-established hierarchies. There's a whole lot to be said for starting small, and learning by working with the grass-roots organizations to build your experience.

The Festival opened my eyes to the television industry as a business. . . and I saw a way to expand my work into the "mainstream" while continuing my focus on positive change.

MOVING TO THE MAINSTREAM

It's been almost thirty years now. I started a Company in addition to the non-profit society. The obligations of a large, growing family precluded a move to a large center like Toronto or Los Angeles, but I have been quietly successful producing hours of international award-winning televisions programming while supporting my family. And I have been able to remain true to my original intention of using media to create positive social change. One highlight of my career since then was the prestigious **Humanitas Prize** in Hollywood for film and television writing – intended to promote human dignity, meaning, and freedom.

RESULTS

Sometimes, of course, I have doubted myself. Would I have been of more use to the world if I had continued my career as a social worker? For all the resources, time and effort we put into a film, it is still really no more than an ephemeral moment in time. It engages the audience for a few minutes – and then it's gone. Might that money have been better spent supporting a family, building a school, buying medicines?

Filmmakers are story tellers – and stories are the most powerful force in the world. And we have the crucial added power of visual messaging. Viewers can empathize and identify with the characters they see on film. They can form "relationships" with them. They can enter and immerse themselves in entire new worlds. The actions and emotions they see played out on the screen are powerfully embedded in their brains.

We all know how athletes use video to train for improved performance –

what they see on screen becomes imprinted into their brain – becomes part of their own action. Watching stories of kindness, courage, perseverance, transformation, hope, heroism and more can, and does, fundamentally move audiences towards adopting those attributes themselves. Of course, the inverse is equally true, and mightily dangerous. It demonstrates vividly how essential it is to ensure the widest possible distribution of positive programming on all platforms, traditional and new media.

As filmmakers, we send our work out into the ether. Usually we do not hear an audience's applause. We cannot know how many people it ultimately reaches, but I have a few treasured stories that show me how effective we CAN be.

Here's just one example:
Over the years I have made seven different films on various aspects of domestic violence – through the lens of children, woman, men, and the elderly, etc. They have been sold all over the world and garnered thousands of dollars in sales revenue for the organizations that commissioned them.

I once got a phone call from a stranger. He found it hard to speak. He said it had taken him months to find out how to reach me in order to say thank you. He had been for many years emotionally and physically abusive to his wife. He had been charged, spent time in prisons and had countless hours of counseling, but it was not until he saw a film I had made (this one *for* men) that he could acknowledge what he was doing. "Suddenly I saw myself on the screen … suddenly I couldn't hide any more from what I was doing… It affected me profoundly. But I also want to thank you because you didn't leave me there – in despair – you showed me a way I could change. And now after many months and much hard work, I can say that I have."

I also know we can create change through programming less obviously targeted at social issues.

As Executive Producer and lead Director, I am currently in pre-production on our third season of a food documentary series – *Moosemeat and Marmalade*. The series features a Cree Indian bush cook – Art Napoleon, and a British gourmet chef, Dan Hayes.

In each episode one host takes the lead and takes us on an adventure to hunt, forage and then cook various wild ingredients. One episode might find us hunting wild buffalo in Northern Canada while the next will be a pheasant shoot on an English country estate. Along the way, Art and Dan explore each other's culture and traditions. The mismatched hosts share a love of food, respect for the environment and desire to foster sustainable food production. They have a lot of fun teasing each other and making fun of each other's foibles. It's a popular, fun show – but it has deeper meaning.

Canada has just concluded a four-year long Truth and Reconciliation Commission trying to confront the many wrongs inflicted on our indigenous population by the colonists and to bring healing and reconciliation to the country. *Moosemeat and Marmalade* is reconciliation in action in an indirect, light-hearted format. As Art may quip, "Boy, these geese just find a piece of land they like with good food and move right in to stay – bit like white folks!" and Dan takes the point in good spirit. But at the same time, exposure to both their heritages and cultures creates growing understanding and respect for each other. Our fan mail demonstrates the effectiveness of this approach when viewers of all races not only comment on how much they love the show, but also note their new appreciation and understanding of other cultures.

CURRENT WORK

A recent feature documentary looks at the social impact of brain injury. I became aware of this issue through volunteer work at a local non-profit organization. I was stunned by a presentation by the Director of Brain Injury Services. He quoted recent surveys of prison populations from the USA to the UK and Norway, that indicated that between 60-80% of their prison populations had a history of brain injury. And the majority of these injuries were sustained BEFORE they engaged in criminal behavior.

I had to look further into this unsettling information. The statistics were compelling. 53 percent of the homeless have brain injuries. After brain injuries, 90 percent of marriages end in divorce, self-medication through substance abuse is rampant, and the suicide rate increases fourfold and the incidence of brain injury among juvenile offenders is very high.

More than 1.7 million traumatic brain injuries (TBI's) occur annually in the US alone, and while every TBI is different, many after-effects are common. They take a grim toll, leading to depression, substance abuse, addiction, crime and divorce. The cost to society is immeasurable, yet once the brain injury survivor leaves hospital there is very little help out there. Thankfully, increasing concern about head injuries in sports has cast a spotlight on brain injury – but there is still very little media about the social impact. I knew I had to make a film about it and spread the message: broken lives can be rebuilt and brains refreshed through new approaches to helping survivors through science, and through changes in social attitudes as well as legal reforms.

The Telus Fund helps finance film and media that enhances healthy outcomes for Canadians, and I was successful in securing a production grant from them. During the two years making the film, I met some extraordinary visionaries working in the field both in social services and in the judiciary. And I was fortunate to follow the stories of two particular individuals from brain injury through resulting addiction, despair, crime and prison to recognition of their brain injury, their subsequent rehabilitation and their re-integration into society – full of hope and determination to help others journey through similar crises.

The resulting film – *A CHANGE OF MIND* - debuts in a special screening hosted by Her Honour, the Lieutenant Governor of British Columbia at BC Government House in November, will broadcast nationally in Canada and is being distributed internationally.

Another current documentary project with Educating Towards Change Society is *A Twentieth Century Passion*. This documents the life journey of holocaust survivor and composer, A. Peter Gary, interweaving haunting refrains from the world premiere of his oratorio in memory of the 6 million Jews massacred in the Second World War.

The story of Peter's fate at the hands of the Nazis becomes the personal story that epitomizes the experience of millions. One terrible Christmas Eve, Peter and his mother – along with 300 others – were taken in trucks to woods near the border with Poland; lined up, naked, on the edge of a ravine and mowed down with machine–guns. Peter's mother jumped in front of him, pushing him down the ravine. Peter and three others survived and made their way to Poland. Peter was smuggled into the Warsaw ghetto, but when the Ghetto was taken he was transported first to

Majdanek then Dachau and ultimately Bergen-Belsen. He was liberated by the British Army on his 21st birthday. He weighed 76 pounds.

Immediately after the war, Peter received his Ph.D. in Ethnomusicology from the Sorbonne. Immigration to the U.S. in 1950 proved a challenge to a young composer. A short stint in Hollywood at MGM ended when the studio went under. Eventually, after obtaining an MD, he went into the rehab business. But he continued to write music – including A 20th Century Passion – music and libretto.

Peter retired to Victoria, BC where he began an indefatigable commitment to the education of young people about the evils of racism, ultimately speaking to over 66,000 young people. Peter's wife promised when they married nine years ago that Peter would see the oratorio performed before he died; *A Twentieth Century Passion* premiered October 17, 2016 in Jerusalem, sadly just a scant three weeks after, Peter died.

His message will resonate through his music and through this film. Peter believed he owed it to the Jewish children who died and to future generations to speak out against hate and to teach tolerance and understanding:

> *"We must stamp out hate for our children. We must believe that we can and will do better."*

THE FUTURE

This belief propels me to my new adventure helping friend and colleague Philippa Steel with her new creation – an animated feature for children: The **DFNDRZ** is a secret gang of five discouraged kids of disparate ethnic and social backgrounds who live in the Pacific Northwest. And have pledged themselves as eco-warriors to protect the land of the Spirit Bear.

The project lends itself to development across all platforms, from feature animation film plus games using the totems and wonderful First Nations stories and legends for inspiration, to web series, TV series and events.

Development is initially at a grass roots level through the formation of a DFNDRZ website and club with free membership, together with local contests for short videos and/or environmentally-oriented projects by children and social media participation.

We're just getting started but we are committed to a hopeful future!

Start small and have faith that things can be changed for the good to benefit us all one step at a time... then another... and another ...

About Hilary

Over the last 25 years, Hilary Pryor, President of May Street Productions, has achieved an impressive reputation as a creative director, writer and producer of inspiring, award-winning broadcast programming on CBC, CTV, Discovery, Turner Network Television, KCTS, Channel Four, Vision TV, Knowledge Network, TVO, APTN, Animal Planet, among others.

Highlights of her career have been the prestigious **Humanitas Prize** in Hollywood for film and television writing intended to promote human dignity, meaning, and freedom and the Japan Prize – Maeda Award for innovative direction.

Hilary's acclaimed television documentaries on social issues have twice been Gemini nominated, received three Chris Awards and three Silver Apples in the U.S. and the Wilbur Award from the Religion Communications Council. Her children's series have won consecutive Awards of Excellence from the Alliance for Children's Television and have broadcast around the world.

Currently Hilary is the Executive Producer and lead director of the award-winning food documentary series, *Moosemeat and Marmalade*, now gearing up for its third season. She recently completed a documentary -- *A Change Of Mind* -- on the social impact of brain injury which debuts in a special screening at Government House in November.

CHAPTER 14

GIVING YOURSELF PERMISSION

5 STEPS TO MAKE IT HAPPEN

BY BETTINA RODRIGUEZ AGUILERA

It seems to be the trend these days to reexamine and try to understand "why" you are not where you want to be. You often see stories of someone that made their dreams a reality and you tell yourself, "why not me." You give yourself a pep talk and assure yourself that this time, "I am going to do this." You get yourself all wound-up and then…life happens. You allow your job, your family, your kids, your car, your significant other, your friends, your whatever, to take over your time and your life.

You are not alone in falling into this cycle. This happens to the best people with the best of intentions. But change starts by giving yourself permission to make it happen. So, the next question is how do you take your dreams off the back burner and actually make them a reality?

Let's start with these five simple steps. While nothing in life is easy, we can begin a process to work towards the life you want. You have to put yourself in a mindset to give yourself permission to focus on you and this process. You must believe in the reality that you can and will make this happen.

Whatever that might be is not as crucial as internalizing the following five steps and making them your own. Once you follow the process, you

133

can adapt it to whatever you desire, visualize the process and crystallize your hopes and dreams.

Are you ready? Here we go. . .

1) Make a commitment to yourself

Your life is often a series of commitments and responsibilities to other people. You have made a million promises, be it finishing that special project at work or taking your kids to a sporting event, and the list continues. But, what about a commitment to yourself?

Yes, you! This means writing yourself in as a meeting in your calendar and setting a reminder on your electronic device or your agenda. This first step includes taking seriously the need to set aside time for the fulfillment of your dreams. In the beginning, this one-on-one meeting with yourself might just be time to allow yourself to think.

Don't think you have time? Well, now is the time to create the space in your life for yourself. Get up fifteen minutes earlier or go to bed later, whatever works for you. The important thing is to take yourself seriously. Make yourself a promise to give yourself the same respect you have given to your other commitments.

2) Override the fear of failure or success

Although you might not have thought of it, fear of success is sometimes more powerful than fear of failure. Many of us subconsciously trigger our own failure because our comfort zone among our friends, our familiar settings, give us a coziness we do not want to let go. It is your safe zone. Success might mean leaving what is familiar. That can be scary.

At the same time, there is the fear of failure. The questions of self-doubt:
- *What if I don't make it?*
- *Am I prepared enough?*
- *I feel that someone is going to see right through me.*
- *I might lose everything!*
- *Am I an imposter?*

Failure is impossible
~ Susan B. Anthony

You only learn lessons on how to do it better next time. The only way society advances is because someone took a risk to follow their persistent inner voice telling them to take the opportunity, to be creative, to take the plunge.

Now is the time to go ahead and do it. You just might surprise yourself for what you can accomplish.

3) Convince yourself you will make it happen

What would happen if you would put dirty water in your car instead of high-octane gas? It would not work properly. Then what makes you think that if you fill your head with bad thoughts and self-doubt that you will be able to believe in yourself or have anyone believe in you? Studies have shown that we talk to ourselves 12,000- 60,000 times a day and of that, 80% is negative.

We are our own worst enemy. That has to STOP right now. The next time you talk bad to yourself, pinch yourself and stop. Bring it to the conscious mind, catch yourself and say, "I will make this happen." Say it for 21 days straight, then it will become a habit. Do this and the beauty of your confidence will shine through and positive things will follow your positive thoughts.

4) Set a Time frame

Giving yourself a time frame is crucial. Dreams are the first step to making "it" happen. Yet, ideas without action will evaporate like the mist of a cloud. Setting a timeline for your ideas, beginning and end, will mark your day and make it real.

Because you have never done this before you may wonder, "When should I start and how long will it take?" The first step is always the hardest. To begin, set a time, if you have to adjust it, do so, but stick to your plan.

Remember that time is your most valuable resource. Time is free to you and everybody has the same amount every day. How you use it will determine your future. How you balance it will determine your life.

I want you to think of time as money, actual liquid cash. Decide how you will spend it, who you are going to give it to, and how you'll prioritize what is important to you. One trick is if it does not help you reach your goal then don't spend your time doing it.

Create a clear time frame to reach each step towards your goal that will lead you to achieve your dream. Make each step small, and realistic, so you can be successful, this will motivate you to keep on going. Write down your goals and look at them every day.

One very important thing, don't forget the first step to "make a commitment to yourself." Treat yourself as your most important client, which means don't reschedule your own appoint; be sure to make that time a priority. If you do not respect yourself, or your allotted time, that will be reflective of the success of your ultimate goal.

5) Tell everyone

Peer pressure, it worked in high school and still works today, but now use it in a positive way. Once you know what you are doing and when your expected outcome will be, spread the news.

Personal branding is key in our current society, tell other people about your project. When you walk into a room, make your project known to others – to the point that people will associate you with your dream. Create enthusiasm and expectations. People will begin to ask you, *'how is your project going?'* They will ask you about your efforts and you will visualize your success. You cannot let yourself and all these people down that have trusted you and your dream. That will give you that added push to give it all you have to bring it to fruition, and be able to share your success with all your fans.

Life happens to everyone, and I would like to share with you a personal experience that I went through, and how this process was applied.

I was in my mid-thirties, married with two small children. I had a full-time job in government as a troubleshooter cutting bureaucratic red tape, and loved it. My mother and father were very much part of my life. Things were good.

One day, my department received a notice that it was being downsized from a staff of 35 to 4 people. The good news was that I was one of the lucky ones that kept my job. Shortly after, the four of us got sick, I had severe earaches and my right arm had to be placed in a sling due to a pinched nerve. It turned out that I had been clenching my jaw at night because of stress and I had snapped the small bones in my face and had TMJ (Temporo-Mandibular Joint disorder) which meant I had to have open face surgery to sew my facial joints together. My employer placed me on leave without pay. My husband and I separated and he left town. My father died and I needed to help take care of my mother and my kids. I could not speak properly because the facial surgery left me with a lot of pain and forced me to wear a large metal machine around my face that opened and closed my jaw. I could not write or type. A social worker came and told me to apply for disability. I refused, but I had to find a way to support my family and my two small children.

At that moment, I knew I had to make a choice and I made a commitment to myself. I wasn't going to give up, and instead I would re-invent myself using the cards I had been handed. Now I had to give myself a timeline. I knew the bills were mounting and had a window of three months, at most, to change my situation. I had to use what I had, which was my government experience and my communication skills.

That year a hurricane hit my hometown and thousands lost their homes and businesses. While watching the news of the devastation, and people desperate for answers, I knew that I could help.

I decided that I had one thing that was still intact, my brain. I found out there was a women's business meeting and decided to go. I stood up at the meeting to introduce myself and said I could help anyone cut through government red tape.

An accountant attending the meeting came up to me and said that she had a client that needed assistance starting a beauty salon and asked if I could help them. Another woman in the meeting offered to rent me workspace and agreed to sign an IOU, but if I couldn't pay in two weeks, I would leave. I immediately got to work, and went to visit what would become my first client, Leo's Beauty Salon. I quickly solved his problems and got paid. I then paid my rent and printed out business cards for $9.99 and went to my next networking meeting at the chamber of commerce. I was determined to make it happen.

People started calling me to help them with issues relating to the hurricane and seeking assistance filling out government disaster loan paperwork. I had never done a business loan, but I did know government. I created a plan and visited with the officials who approved the loans, and used that new knowledge to create a process to secure loans.

I was invited to a local radio station to discuss what I was doing, and offered advice on how and where people could get help. From there my business grew. I was doing 20-30 loans a month, helping with government issues and hosting trainings on government and believing in myself. I moved into a larger office, hired associates and turned my life around. I was still going through two additional open-face surgeries and physical therapy, but regardless, I had to find the time to make this work.

That choice to give myself permission and not to give up, propelled me to start helping women and men on how to internalize the five steps into their lives. I started my own company, opened the first non-profit incubator/executive offices for women in USA, guiding others on how to start their business and believe in themselves. I became an economic developer, elected official, developed the Miami-Dade College's Women's Institute – Women Empowering Leadership Certificate course. I became a playwright and a public speaker, trainer, consultant and coach. You see, it doesn't matter what life throws at you as long as you GIVE YOURSELF PERMISSION and apply the five steps, you will MAKE IT HAPPEN. Now sit down and map your future.

About Bettina

Bettina Rodriguez Aguilera has over 25 years of professional experience in business development, leadership building, and women's issues. She is a highly sought-after speaker, trainer, coach and consultant as well as a policy expert, providing insights to the media in English and Spanish. Bettina is a former elected official, economic developer, author of 15 training modules, as well as the Women's Leadership Workbook and the founder of the Miami Dade College's Women Institute, where she wrote the curriculum and teaches leadership and business skills. Currently Bettina is the president and founder of Bettinara Enterprises, Inc.-Leadership and Business Institute.

Personal Development
Bettina is a Cuban exile, immigrating to the United States as an infant with her mother and older brother. She began working at the age of 13 to help with family expenses, her father was a Cuban political prisoner and wasn't reunited with the family until she was 17 years old. Bettina graduated high school at the age of 16 and put herself through college by starting her first business at 18. She graduated from Miami Dade College and continued at Florida International University (FIU) earning degrees in Psychology and Social Work. She holds certificates from the University of Miami on Budget and Financial Management, in Leadership from Harvard through the National Hispana Leadership Institute (NHLI) fellowship, as well as the Center for Creative Leadership and Stephen Covey University.

World of Business
Her business success and individual coaching helped launch an international career, training government officials and corporations at home and abroad. Bettina has assisted over 800 companies become certified to receive government contracts and/or business loans. She developed and taught the first leadership certificate program in Spanish for the University of Miami's Koubeck Center in the 1990's. Bettina has developed and conducted training programs for Albania, Bosnia Herzegovina, Lithuania, Libya, Ghana, Argentina, Mexico, Dominican Republic, United States and other nations.

In 1993, she began a non-profit to inspire and mentor entrepreneurs at the New Woman Entrepreneur Center. The center provided incubator offices, training and workshops, these efforts assisted over 600 start-up small businesses and was the first of its kind. She assisted the opening of similar programs in Ghana and Lithuania.

Recognitions

Throughout her career Bettina has been acknowledged for her efforts, including FIU's Distinguished Alumnae, an American flag erected above the US Capital, inducted in the League of United Latin American Citizens (LULAC) Women's Hall of Fame, recognized as the former Florida state director of LULAC. She is a board member of Safe Space Women's Shelter Foundation, FIU Women's Center, and the Rotary Club among others. She received a letter of recognition from Secretary General of the United Nations, Ban Ki-Moon for the passage of the First Resolution in the Nation of Orange Day – to end violence against women and girls. Vanidades - Han Triunfado, Cromos-Distinguished figure, *Hispanic Magazine*, *Miami Herald* Editorial - Passing along her experience – as well as Proclamations and Certificates of Recognition from local and international organizations.

Bettina is a proud mother of two grown children and a grandmother.

Bettina may be reached at: www.bettinaraenterprises.com for public speaking and consulting.

CHAPTER 15

THE POWER OF "LET GO"

BY MARK MCMANUS

[Acknowledgment: First and foremost, I want to thank the two most important people in my life: my beautiful wife Megan and my incredible mother Jill, without whose support none of my successes would have been possible.]

My goal is to add value to you. However, I have to start by saying that this chapter is not for everyone. Here's the test; if you are a leader, entrepreneur, CEO or executive and you have a fixed mindset and believe that the way you've always done it is the only way and you've got it all figured out, then there's no need to continue any further. However, if you have a growth mindset, meaning that you're open to the idea that you may not have it all figured out and there may be a better way to *lead* your company, then read on, I hope that you're able to get something from this chapter.

I've spent many years trying to get this one point through to entrepreneurs, CEOs and leaders at all levels…LET GO. This chapter will either be a series of checked boxes, or it will be a stark reality check. I'm not here to give you "fluff." I'm here to add value to you. Too many times I've seen first-hand that entrepreneurs, CEO's and leaders believe that they know better or that they are the exception to this principle. Time after time the results are the same. The pain has to be felt before they believe that they don't have to, and can't continue to, do everything and micromanage every aspect of their team and their business.

Let me first give you some background about me. It was May 19th, 1999 just after 11 pm in pitch black darkness with my head down, forehead touching my knees on a bus with 67 other civilians when I arrived on board Marine Corps Recruit Depot, San Diego. The first words I heard were "You are now aboard Marine Corps Recruit Depot - San Diego, receiving barracks, building 622. From now on, the last words out of your mouth at all times will be 'Sir!' Is that understood?" "YES, SIR!" we all erupted. "I said IS THAT UNDERSTOOD?" "YES, SIR!" we yelled even louder than the first time."

It was at that moment that my journey and passion for leading, being a part of a team and my understanding of the "people first" mentality truly began.

In total, I spent nine years in the Marine Corps; five years as an aviation mechanic and four years as a Marine Corps Drill Instructor. During that time, I was privileged to work side-by-side with and lead thousands of Marines from many different walks of life. The experiences I had during that nine years alone were enough to write a book about. Well, that may be the next one on the list.

Following my time in the Marine Corps, I went to school and received an Associate's degree in Accounting and proceeded to try my hand at it. In January of 2008, I quickly got a position as an Accountant at an Architecture firm in La Jolla, CA. Long story short, after one long year of what felt like Groundhog Day, I quickly realized that this was not for me. I always have and always will measure my career satisfaction by the impact that I have on people, not on profits. When you take care of people, the profits will follow, but we'll talk more about that later in the chapter.

Once I realized that accounting was not something I wanted to pursue as my career path, I knew I needed to learn a tangible skill that would allow me to get a foot in the door of business. This was at a time when YouTube was becoming mainstream, and anything could be learned only by hitting Google and looking. I spent about a year educating myself about web design, web development and marketing, while at the same time finishing up the classes required to get a bachelor's degree in Information Technology. To be honest, I could have taught the classes, but I knew that I needed the piece of paper to legitimize my abilities. I had learned enough to pick up a handful of small business contracts to build and maintain their web presence. The money was good, but there was still something missing, the people.

In August of 2008, I had received an email from another former Drill Instructor and Sergeant Major in the Marine Corps that said he was heading up the residential side of a boarding school in southern California, and he was looking to bring on a former drill instructor to help turn it around. The school housed children from the 6th grade all the way to young adults in the 12th grade. I was going to be in charge of a section that housed 9th through 12th graders. This was a new leadership challenge for me. In a military environment, for the most part, the team you lead has a level of obligation to execute the orders which they are given, but teenagers have no reason to listen to what you have to say. For any given child, the cost of attending the boarding school was around $35,000 a year. With few exceptions, the majority of these kids came from very wealthy families and had a sense of entitlement. Their respect had to be earned. Sixth months into the position, the section I had the privilege of leading had broken several long-standing records, and were amongst the top candidates in the school. To this day, I still receive emails and messages about how the two years I spent with them, and teaching them a sense of responsibility, ownership, and respect had changed many of their lives.

After two years at the boarding school, I relocated to Dallas, TX where I interviewed for the first position with a company that would allow me to put my skillset to work and lead people. I was hired on as a Marketing Assistant in November of 2011. By 2012, I was the Director of Marketing with a team of six. In 2014, I was the Vice President of Operations leading a team of 26, and by January of 2016, I was the COO with the privilege of leading a fast-growing team of 50+. During this time, we earned a spot on the INC. 500/5000 list of fastest-growing companies for five consecutive years.

I have since relocated to Atlanta, and am currently working with a fast-growth technology company with 150+ team members. I continue to have a passion for creating an opportunity for those around me and continuously strive to create a people-first culture.

Why do I tell you all of that? It is to paint a picture that I have had the opportunity and privilege to lead many individuals and teams from diverse backgrounds with many different objectives. The one thing that I've distilled down from all of my experience is that the more you "let go," the more you will ultimately get back – in both growth of the people on your team and ultimately, the growth of your business. 78% of companies in the Fortune 1000 and 81% of manufacturing organizations currently deploy such "empowered," "self-directed" or "autonomous" teams.

Although there are many ways to begin to build your "let go" muscle, I am going to give you eight of the principles you can start to put into practice today:

1. **Lead by example:** Before you start to delegate responsibility to your team, take a hard look at yourself in the mirror and evaluate how you are currently handling the responsibility that you're going to hand off. Are you executing in a manner which you would find acceptable by that person? If the answer is yes, you're well on your way. If the answer is no, start setting the example that you want in your team. The threat: if you operate under the principle of "do as I say, not as I do," your team will begin to pick up on your bad habits, and when it comes time for them to take charge and lead initiatives, they are going to do what they have witnessed.

2. **Credible accountability:** Know enough to be able to hold the empowered team accountable while maintaining their confidence in you. While you don't have to have a college degree in every aspect of business, you should have enough understanding in each area of your business to be able to hold the team accountable to the result and to be able to help alleviate bottlenecks that they may encounter. Having a basic understanding of any given area of the business allows you not to have the answer necessarily, but to know where to look.

3. **Your standard is not their standard:** As an entrepreneur, you can hope they care as much about the business as you do, but don't expect them to, and don't get pissed off when they seem as if they don't care. If you haven't given them the ownership of their responsibility, don't hold them accountable for the outcome as the owner. Create a standard for the team to uphold that aligns with the mission of your company, and make sure that their compensation aligns with their

responsibilities and results. Don't expect your team to be "bought in" for the future, if you haven't made it clear how the company's future translates to their financial future. Here's a quick example: Two companies, both have a great culture and work environment. One underpays and doesn't give "ownership" to the results. The other offers compensation that is aligned to responsibility and gives tangible "ownership" to the company's future. Which company would you rather work with? Don't have a double standard.

4. **Surprise and delight:** Give them a break, surprise them. Once you have handed off and delegated responsibility to your team, one of the best opportunities you have is to surprise and delight your team. I like to call this "interrupting the pattern." A few of the ways that I've done this in the past is by telling the team to wear comfortable shoes on a Friday and not telling them why only to have a huge bus show up and take them to an amusement park for the day. This type of thing creates memorable moments that will live throughout the company's culture for years to come. They will post it on social media for the world to see; which by the way will help in your recruiting efforts. You will have time to create these types of magic moments when you aren't busy micromanaging every aspect of the business.

5. **Pay attention to overload:** It's always a great feeling when you see your team choose to work after the whistle blows. You see that as a sign of their buy-in to the company and their passion for accomplishing the mission at hand. It's true; your "A" players will make an effort to put in more hours and sacrifice more for the sake of the mission. However, you must pay close attention to the frequency and rationale for the extra hours. The minute it starts to become a table stake, you've failed. You don't want to create a culture of time=buy-in. It's your responsibility to ensure that work/life balance is not a buzz word, but something that you are going to hold them accountable for. Burnout is real, and it's the fastest way to drive an "A" player to the brink.

6. **Practice, practice, practice:** Delegation takes practice. As with anything, the more you do it, the better you will get. As Malcolm Gladwell says: *To truly be great at something you have to put in your 10,000 hours.* If you are having trouble knowing where to start, ask

yourself this question as you approach any task, responsibility or project. "Do I change the outcome?" If the answer is no, let it go. Once you've delegated those responsibilities, the next question to ask yourself is, "Do I enjoy doing this?" Again, if the answer is no, let it go. You should be doing the things that you enjoy, and things in which you can actually change the outcome.

7. **Maintain the org:** If you've always operated as the "go-to" person in your company for all questions about everything, you've probably felt like there was a revolving door to your office. This is one of the symptoms of not delegating responsibility and ownership to lower levels of leadership on your team. As you begin to hand-off ownership to your team, you will see that the revolving door will not stop immediately. It will take discipline for you to maintain the new structure of responsibility, but it is one of the most valuable things you can do for your leadership team. When they come to you, the first question should be, "Have you ran this by xxx first?"

Here's an example of how I would explain this to the company. I would tell them to try and solve the problem at the lowest level first. Take a football team for example. If you are a quarterback and you need a new mouthpiece, who do you go to? You go to the equipment manager, not the head coach or the owner of the team. If you're the quarterback and you want to run a new play, who do you go to? The equipment manager is probably not qualified to give feedback on a new play, and the owner will probably wonder why he's paying the head coach if he has players coming to him to talk about new plays. The head coach would be your man. Now, if you have a strategy about how to improve the salary cap and make room for negotiations with a free-agent from another team, then the owner would most likely be the "go-to" person for that conversation.

This example usually sets a good framework for understanding how and when to solve various types of challenges at the lowest level where possible. Once your team sees you respecting the organizational and reporting structure, they will begin to do the same, and your leadership team and mid-level managers will feel a sense of empowerment and ownership like never before, because they know you believe in their abilities.

8. **If not for you, for your team:** If you don't begin to let go of responsibility and ownership for the sake of your own sanity, do it for your people. People by nature want to do good. They want to have an impact and do something that matters. There is much research that points to this being especially true for millennial's, but I believe it spans all ages. No one wakes up every morning and goes to a job where they tell themselves, "Man, I hope I don't do anything that matters today."

In Summary

To wrap this up, I want you to remember always to focus on the people first, and trust me, profits will come. There's never been a company in the history of the world that has had a significant impact without leveraging the collective intelligence and ingenuity of a collective group. Even the great Steve Jobs was quoted as saying "It doesn't make sense to hire smart people and then tell them what to do; we hire smart people so they can tell us what to do."

I hope you were able to take away something from this chapter that you are going to implement in your business to start letting go and watching the magic happen. I would love to hear how some of these principles work for you in execution or ways that you've begun to exercise the power of "let go." If you have any questions or just want to talk through tactical scenarios of "letting go," you can email me. You can also keep an eye out for the release of my book, *The Power of LET GO: How empowering your team will drive exponential growth in your company and give you back your life.*

Here's to you and the power of "let go."

About Mark

Mark McManus has a passion for leading teams. Mark also has a passion for coaching leaders, entrepreneurs and CEO's in his "people first" leadership style. Having been in numerous leadership roles throughout his entire adulthood, Mark has had the opportunity to understand what works, and more importantly what doesn't work, in leading high production teams.

Mark has had a fast-track career with promotions through a series of increasingly responsible management and leadership positions. Honored with numerous commendations and awards for outstanding leadership, general management, and operations excellence, Mark has made his focus providing opportunity and adding value to those around him. He is also certified in Real Colors®, a personality testing system that helps people learn to work together, breaking down organizational silos and increasing productivity.

Mark McManus joined Commissions Inc. in October of 2016 as the head of Business Development and Marketing. Prior to joining Commissions, Inc., Mark served as the COO of The National Association of Expert Advisors (NAEA) where his "people first" approach to leadership and his focus on teamwork and rapid execution helped drive year over year growth of the business, earning NAEA five consecutive years on the INC. 500/5000 list of fastest growing companies.

Mark has over eleven years of experience in leading teams and driving initiatives in multiple facets of business growth. Mark also had the privilege of honing his leadership skills while serving nine years in the United States Marine Corps as a CH-46 Engine Mechanic, Marine Corps Drill Instructor, and Combat Water Survival Instructor.

As a speaker, Mark has shared the stage with some of the top entrepreneurs and small business influencers in the world, such as Darren Hardy, Jay Abraham and Nick Nanton.

Mark has also participated in masterminds with some of the top companies in the country such as Infusionsoft's Elite Mastermind led by Infusionsoft CEO Clate Mask and The War Room led by Digital Marketer's CEO Ryan Deiss.

Mark currently resides in Atlanta, GA with his beautiful wife Megan, and their incredible two-year-old son, Gavin.

You can connect with Mark at:
- mark@thepowerofletgo.com.
- mark@markjmcmanus.com
- www.twitter.com/markjmcmanus
- www.facebook.com/TheMarkMcManus

CHAPTER 16

COMPASSION IS GOD'S SCIENCE

BY PAIVI LAPPALAINEN

God's Compassion is the oldest science of over 3000 years. Ordinary people achieve remarkable results.

- Have we forgotten that every one of us comes to this earth as a human being first from the love of a mother in the womb?
- What has happened to our society?
- Why is success more important than human kindness?

I learned as a very young child the power of "Compassion is God's Science."

Somehow, in my one-year-old body, I was diagnosed with childhood Leukemia. I was admitted to St. Mary's Hospital in Toronto for treatment. Mom was with me 7am-7pm, leaving my sister with babysitters. A strange place this hospital is; all the children in beds, fighting for their lives. Dad was a taxi driver and a spiritual leader at the time. He cared much for his family. Dad gave me what is called a Priesthood blessing before I was admitted to the hospital, as is the practice.

As parents, they had so many questions: What were they to do? How is this possible? Will she live? I was in and out of the hospital for about a year. Dad gave me another blessing in between. Then every parent's nightmare became a reality: The Doctor gave my parents a 24-hour prognosis of my death. They wondered, how could this be? We did all the right things. Two congregations even fasted and prayed for my recovery. There was faith in every footstep. The next morning, Mom heard a voice that whispered, "If you bring your daughter home from the hospital, she'll be well." Imagine what may have crossed her mind. Is this true, could she still live? She chose to discuss this with Dad. Together, using Dad's taxi car, they wrapped me in white and snuck me out of the hospital during the morning shift change.

The nurses and doctors panicked, they called my parents to see if I was there. When they discovered I was safe at home, the Doctor asked, "Why did you bring her home?" Mom simply replied, "If she is going to die, let her die at home." Mom got the fever down and two days later there was absolutely no trace of leukemia left in my mortal body. It took two weeks to regain my strength. No one seemed to know exactly how I was healed of the Leukemia. Yet, Mom noticed a change in me. I had a lack of concentration and a fear of women.

This gives us a reason to perhaps examine my life and why I can even be considered a broken soul. For in order to be repaired, there must have been something broken, right? Also we need to understand how the Savior became part of my life. Is it possible for His loving power to heal us today? On the outside, we did very normal things. We grew up as a family of six. At a young age for us, our parents were very active in church. They taught us that the Savior is real. Some of my fondest memories growing up were at Christmas time and how our family celebrated the birth of Jesus Christ on Christmas Eve. As children, we used to act out parts of the Nativity story. We also served the Lord as a family on building missions, one in Peterborough, Canada and the other in Tampere, Finland. Friends say I was a kind, quiet child. Dad said I was easy to raise. Perhaps I learned obedience very young. My solace as a teenager was journaling. We had the normal upbringing of school, church friends, play, piano lessons, pets, etc.

My married life became beyond challenging with a spouse who chose to go against his beliefs and live a double life. He began using substances, being abusive, engaging others. I, so foreign to his new world and even poverty, carried out my purpose quietly. It was during this time I was at an NLP Master Practitioner Training when flashbacks emerged. I felt stunned, frozen, not sure whether to flee or stand still. I realized I was just as the kids I served. I was raped and beaten in that hospital while suffering from leukemia. Yet, I always knew my parents loved me. How could I handle this? I chose to utilize Time Empowerment and seek a Priesthood blessing, which in my belief with the proper authority is the power to act in the name of God. It worked. The words I received were, "And now all pain in your past is removed." I felt this as all pain was removed.

In 2013, I truly understood poverty when after my first book signing, I temporarily lost sight in my right eye; well, I almost lost my eye altogether. I had two invasive surgeries and seven laser treatments with no pain. During an energy alignment session, we uncovered the root cause of my residual challenge being that first trauma in the hospital as a child. In compassion, Dr. H. Hudson stated, "I want this chapter in your life closed." And thus it was. Because I have known hardship and have received compassion as well, I can personally attest to compassion's healing wonders. This is the understanding which led me to Mario and compelled me to help him.

Are you ready to be inspired?

On Friday May 6, 2016, my client and unofficially adopted son, Mario (who is an adult), returned home after experiencing a miracle. Mario has a seemingly impossible mental challenge known as Paranoid Schizophrenia. The night before he had an episode that had required him to be gently removed from our home by a kind church leader in order to regroup.

When he arrived home the following morning we sat down in the dining room to talk.

"Paivi, I realized that, though I consider you family, I was treating you like my family who were mean to me," he shared. "Yet I realized you are always kind and loving to me, I remembered when I was a baby how my Mom loved me and held me."

Then I asked my son to look me in the eyes. He did. I asked him, "Do you feel the Savior's love when you look me in the eyes?"

"Yes," my son said.

My response was, "You broke the curse son, welcome back." He said it felt good to be back.I was able to hug him for the first time in years and truly feel him hugging me back. This is a scientific miracle.

The bond of a mother and child is so powerful that it broke the curse of abuse that had been weighing on his mind, body and soul for years. Let me provide a little more background on Mario.

At age 13, his family unit, as he had known it, fell apart. From then on he had to raise himself. Imagine a child being raised with much abuse, neglected and lonely, without a bed to call his own. School was Mario's joy and his only sense of accomplishment – he even took Calculus at 13! I met him in 1999 when he was 15, at a Youth Leadership Training he attended through an LA County Probation School. However, we did not stay in touch.

In October 2015, I woke up two days in a row with a song from Les Miserables in my head; to me it was a message that meant bring him home. My son was in Vegas at that time, he was on his knees praying and asking God what to do as he struggled with addiction. He says he received a peaceful feeling so powerful that he will never forget it and then a whisper of instruction to "Call the church and call Paivi." He had lost his phone, but had remembered my website, Humanchampionspirit. com.

On October 30, 2015, I found him in a hospital in Las Vegas with nothing but a T-shirt, jeans and shoes that were causing a fungus on his feet. I put him up in a hotel for three nights. It was there I told him he is a son of God, not an addict. The most important thing to him was to get a pair of black tennis shoes, a white shirt, tie and slacks so he could go to church.

Mario tried to overcome his negative reoccurring thoughts on his own with the following methods:

- Music
- Hospital stay
- Medications
- Drugs
- Alcohol
- Counseling

However, the help I could provide by acting as his mother were better alternatives:

- A bed, a room, clean clothes
- Prayer
- Scriptures
- Church
- Sessions of Joy
- Patience
- Music
- Healthier food
- Service to others
- Accepting compassion

The bottom line was compassion, or the love of a mother, gave him clarity. With compassion, Mario recognized the love he received as an infant and young child. It was simply compassion that brought about his unconscious cognitive realization. There is a science to this.

The love of a mother became his miracle.

44 million people in our country suffer from mental illnesses according to NAMI. Physical, mental, sexual and emotional abuses are a great cause of these. I learned that my son would transfer the thoughts of the drug lords who threatened him to me. His association with family and chaos at home were transferred to me as well. It was a great challenge to maintain consistent love and kindness, a challenge that I accepted. My son received his first bed and his first room. He received shoes that were orthopedic, which helped his back condition. The compassion provided to him through those items and my consistent love in the face of many challenges have made all the difference. It has let him know the joy and immense healing power of a hug – which is a physical manifest of compassion itself.

Human Champion Spirit is about compassion. God is our example. The ability that compassion has to heal the soul and the body is what life is truly all about. Everyone deserves compassion. It is why I help people like my son, Mario and the others listed below:

(a). **Israel** – Our Youth Leadership student was at probation camps at 13, completed his high school requirements by 15, but he was refused graduation. Now has a wife, children and passed his exams as a Sheriff.

(b). **Wendy** – She realized the Savior is always there for her. She opened up with her mother and the next day she was able to speak to her audience with authentic confidence.

(c). **Sarah** – She was gang raped at 19, and in her words, had a "deep depression, wanted to end my life." Sarah is now a Mom and says, "I feel joy, better relationships."

A Mother's love is compassion. God's Compassion is a simple science. At Human Champion Spirit, we believe in "Love, Forgive and Be."

1. **Love** with God's Compassion
2. **Forgive** mending family bonds
3. **Be** trusting in a living Higher Power

About Paivi

A seasoned Human Champion Spirit Guide, who received this role due to her ability to comprehend well the value of a spirit intelligence YOU and this unity with our own physical bodies. Her first overcoming experience was in a battle for life as a child with leukemia. Somehow on her deathbed, she received divine help and in two days there was no medical evidence of any trace of leukemia left in her body. This early experience taught her how faith in a divine power brings about miracles and nothing good is impossible.

Her work with Utah Special Olympics and Director of Handicapped Services at BYU earned her the nomination for Most Outstanding Young Woman of America in the early 80's. She is a two-time nominee for *LA Business Journal, Women Making A Difference*. In 1999, Paivi began a Leadership Training Seminar for Youth in the Juvenile Probation Department of the Los Angeles County that they called Kid's Capital. They were measured with an 80% success rate. Her life experiences in overcoming, rape, torture, poisoning, rejection, ID fraud, stalking in three states, and eye stroke have been for her some spiritual lessons of Joy. With God by her side, she found the answers to many challenges with others – all the while applying the lessons of pure compassion, in no matter what circumstances she found herself or others in.

Paivi is a published author of *The Mustard Tree*, a children's fully illustrated book and audio CD. She is a published poet known for her published work, *Reflection*. She is bold, direct and so compassionate she is known in the North County Special Needs community for her outstanding ability to draw out the joy when others see only the challenge. One boy moved his fingers for the first time in his life. One woman, during college years with down syndrome, sang "Oh Holy Night" in a tenor range. Paivi enjoys using her talents in art, music, sports and voice to draw out the smiles and hidden gifts of others.

Paivi developed an adaptation to Ho'oponopono with permission which she has used to help countless victims of rape and abuse of many forms, to forgive the cruelties of this world. Her clients have realized a greater light within them and become more emotionally self-reliant. Paivi believes that emotional self-reliance is connected to spiritual awareness and even physical joy. She herself went through an isolated stroke in her right eye, two invasive surgeries, seven laser treatments and more, found herself without pain through it all. She also is medication-free and her eyesight is returning in stages. Paivi is graceful and understanding with all people. She has been said to emulate the love the Savior has – even through her eyes.

Paivi Lappalainen is a Certified Trainer NLP Time Empowerment and Human Champion Spirit.

Contact information:
- Enkeliguide@hushmail.com
- http://humanchampionspirit.com

CHAPTER 17

COMATOSE

BY PETRA NICOLL

I am an accumulation of those who went before me—and the people, places and events of my life today—and those yet to come. My desire in writing this story is to inspire others in this world who perhaps ask the same question that I did.

Why am I here and what is my true purpose on earth?

For me, adulthood had many twists and turns, filled with light and darkness. It took me some time to make sense of it all. And it was quite magical, how life events would propel me to identify the repeated life patterns, and to fully accept myself for who I had become—and to utilize my gifts as I discovered my purpose on this earth.

Life laced with chaos and unmet emotional needs, eventually led me to a place of being filled with deep love and contentment. It seemed as if there had always been a plan. There was much drama and trauma—a near-death experience at the age of nine, the sudden and tragic death of my mother, suicide, depression, and realities of war impacted and influenced my life.

What have I learned?

I was led to the Masters of the Far East, the Shamans of North America and Mexico, which awakened me to the realization and the vision that I had been given—to become transformed and more intuitive—which guided me on a journey that I now use as tools to help others. Like the caterpillar becomes the butterfly—it took a metamorphosis to evolve to where I am today—to become transformed, more intuitive, and yes, even psychic, as I moved into a life of deep introspection, and acceptance of what is—a transcendental journey that spanned decades.

Recognizing that life is a gift that has been given to us, it is in our hands to make the best out of it—and dare to believe that we can. Being true to ourselves and soul-centered removes us from the collective mainstream, as it opens the door to our broken heart, finally to reveal to you, and to me, the nectar of this wildly delicious and messy life that moves steadily towards a finish line that leaves you, and those you touch, radically free.

COMATOSE

It was December of 1970, one of the coldest winters Bavaria had seen in years, temperatures dropped to twenty degrees below zero. We lived outside of Munich, Germany, in my hometown of "Markt Schwaben," which was covered by a blanket of shimmering snow.

The plows could barely keep up with the heavy downfall, which greatly amused us children always ready for the next adventure. To us, it was a magical winter wonderland. I was nine years old, dreamy-eyed and full of youthful play and laughter.

My mother had warned me to stay home and take care of my cold, but life was too exciting, and I insisted on spending the night at my fun aunt and uncle's. Their apartment was cold, and I was coughing so much that my ribcage ached, sending shivers running down my spine.

When I got back home, my mother bundled me up in a cozy blanket on the sofa, and in her sweetest voice, kissed my forehead, and played some soft classical music. She gave me some medicine, and left for town with my brother, Wolfgang, to run a quick, urgent errand in town.

I slowly drifted to sleep. Out of the blue, I woke up with such terror, jumping in panic. Desperately gasping for air, I sounded like a barking seal at the circus. I flailed around as my cough worsened.

Between coughs, a strange crow-like noise escaped me—a wheezing sound like the one my friend made when she had an asthma attack. I could feel my chest sink with each gasping breath. Something wasn't right! I touched my ribs; they felt displaced. I was barely conscious.

My body shifted and jolted in spasms again.

Out of dazed desperation, with all my strength I stood up, and raised my arms above my head, desperately hoping to open up my air passages so I could breathe. Each time I attempted to breathe inward, my air-passages tightened even more. I finally gave in.

Suddenly, everything turned quiet and still, just like the snow outside.

A humming sound filled my ears—it was peaceful and quiet; fear and terror left me. I fell to the floor and rolled under the glass coffee table. Eventually, the chest pain stopped. I began drifting toward a bright light— not of this world. I slipped out of consciousness again, withdrawing from my body.

Time passed… My mother's voice called, "Petra, Petra." She pulled me from under the table. Once again, I felt the unbearable tightness in my chest as I gulped for oxygen. She screamed at Wolfgang to keep me upright, commanding him to walk me around the house. In my delirium, I almost fell down the stairs. My poor brother! Immediately, my mother called for my dad to drive us to the nearest hospital in Steinhoering, a town 15 kilometers from us.

At 14-years-old, my mother had been hospitalized there. She had contracted the polio virus and was paralyzed for two years. The worst part, besides the pain, my mother said, was the emotional ache of being locked away there. Unable to hug her own mother, except through a dingy, institutional window, made her feel like a prisoner.

No air to breathe. Not in my body, I floated upward, hovering on the hospital ceiling, not my bed, which felt strange.

During this experience, I witnessed my body from a distance, its every move, my Spirit moved along the walls of the old hospital.

How was this possible?

Later, I would learn this about the hospital—with its roots in dreadful Nazi evil. In 1935, a most feared Nazi, Himmler, created a secret Nazi program called "Lebensborn" in this hospital. Deemed racially pure, young women were taken from their families and isolated in those cavernous walls to meet SS officers, to become pregnant, so that they could bring more "racially pure" into the world. Nazi authorities believed that these Lebensborn children would be purebred Aryans, perfect future SS-leaders (given to the SS to train from birth); these children would become the new nobility that would dominate the world. At least, that was the plan.

"What is happening to me?" I faintly recall asking.

I watched from above my body to see my father standing next to me, holding my hand close to his heart, his tears falling on my lifeless face. I could feel his sadness and aching heart. I knew he didn't think I was going to make it. I wasn't "Petra" in her hospital bed; I was hovering above them, trying to make sense of it all.

My mother, in her red fox coat, sat in the eerie and the sterile corridor outside of my room. She sat on a wooden bench, reading something, black pen in hand, her face pale. She appeared numb with dismay, a horror no mother wants to endure. Somehow, in my out-of-body state, I knew she was signing a document to consent to a dangerous surgery.

I remember thinking… Poor mummy, watching me on the edge of death in the same dreadful place she had to remain while ill with polio in her childhood. Momentarily, I felt as if I was slipping into her body, her mind and spirit—I could feel her sorrow and despair. Her intense emotions came over me in a vibration of dread and sadness.

I then traveled into a room to the next operation, where two doctors in their light green, baggy scrubs, and several nurses, vigorously scrubbed and washed their hands. I had a bird's-eye view. Wherever my attention focused, there I was. I could see clearly and feel what everyone was feeling, as if I was able to slip inside their bodies and read their minds. Experiencing their every emotion, didn't seem odd or scary; I felt calm and neutral, unemotional, as I moved through the corridors.

I remember trying to get their attention, thinking I had called out to my father, "Pappi, Pappi – I'm up here!" Then I said something like, "Don't cry – I'm alright, you don't have to worry about me." I continued, "I'm up here, I'm up here – look up, I am on the ceiling!! I am fine!"
But my Pappi stared at my lifeless body and couldn't hear me calling out.

What is happening to my spirit? Why is my body lying there, yet I am on the ceiling looking down at my body with such a sense of calm? I recall feeling this inner knowing that everything was perfect on those cream-white walls, when, suddenly, my spirit shot through a tunnel much like a vortex of clouds, illuminated by a bright white light.

I was flying like a bird, up, up through the sky. I felt this strange energy project me through the light with such enormous speed. It was as if I was enveloped by this brilliant ray inside and out. The sun was hugely magnified. I felt safe. It was otherworldly and intoxicating to my spirit.

I eventually found myself in an edifice that appeared like a gigantic library with a multitude of floors and books reaching into the vast sky. The joy, love and peace prevailed inside me. Feeling free and incredibly warm from the inside out, the humming sound reverberated throughout this tall library. It all seemed strangely familiar.

In an instant, I stood next to seemingly wise old men. They reminded me of ancient Babylonians or the Franciscan monks in Bavaria, dressed in simple cloaks of white and brown.

One had a hefty, old book in his hand. He read from this leather-bound book. As I stared at their handsome, weathered faces, I felt like I had known them before, and they knew me. I felt I recognized one man in particular. He had the most peaceful and kindhearted face. There was a bluish light emanating from him, and his eyes were so blue and bright that I wanted to get lost inside of them. I recognized Jesus the instant I set eyes on him. I could not conceive of a more loving face and eyes. Jesus and the other elders were talking about my fate, united in their care and concern. We were ONE.

They weren't talking like humans talk. Their conversation carried on telepathically; I could somehow perceive their ideas and deep messages of love. Not a little girl anymore, I felt timeless and one with them. No identity, no borders—I felt truly at home in their affection, their compassion and their deep love. I asked them if I could stay. But, no...

They smiled at me the way a loving father smiles at a daughter... And then it all went black.

The following morning, I woke up in the Intensive Care Unit in a vast room with old, wooden floors. The peace I had just experienced—gone—and I didn't like it. I looked away from the child, and heard the creak of a heavy door, like that of a medieval castle. High-heel shoes echoed down the corridor—and then, the familiar voice of my mother.

I could barely make out what she said: "Herzilein, Herzilein, you made it; I could not live without you!" She kissed my face, and stroked my hair, while my aunt held my hand. I tried to speak, but I couldn't utter a sound or open my eyes.

What happened? Why was I back, and how long was I gone? I had no idea. My entire body was exhausted. Then it happened again. The peace returned, as if God himself was holding me in his arms. It seemed I floated in a warm liquid, and the soothing, buzzing sound was all around. I was terribly sick, my mother still worried, but my trance-like state seemed to envelope me in such a deep bliss that I have very little memory of what went on around me for the rest of my recovery.

One morning at breakfast and not long after I returned home from the hospital, I told my mother about the light and about Jesus, when she gently put her index finger on my lips and said, "Shhhhhh... we will never speak of this, little girls don't talk to Jesus, and they will put you away in an insane asylum if you tell anybody."

Something had shifted inside of me, feeling strangely detached from my family and my life as it was before, wishing I could go home to the place of peace and love forever.

And to quote Maya Angelou —

My mission in life is not merely to survive, but to thrive; and to do so with some passion, some compassion, some humor, and some style!

What is my wish for you? Through my story written on these pages, my intent is to inspire you to find the courage to extract and tell the story that maybe buried deep inside of you!

In doing so, evolving personal acceptance, greater knowledge and understanding, and full recognition of YOUR TRUE PURPOSE on this earth - seen in full, living color.

- Why do "bad" things happen to "good" people?

- Are we the directors of our own movie?

When something bad happens, you have three choices. You can:

1. let it define you
2. let is destroy you
3. let it strengthen you

Through the ups and downs in life, you'll find lessons are learned that will make you grow into who you were meant to be.

- What stories about your past do you remember so vividly?

- What stories and events in your past have you tried to forget?

If you want to transform yourself, and transform your life, you cannot ignore the stories and events that have made you who you are today. Instead, you must embrace them, as difficult as that may be, because they are there, so that you will find your light and your life's purpose.

So, let me help you tell your story! Your storied past holds the code to your universe, to what's deep inside of you.

The Dalai Lama when asked what surprised him the most about humanity, answered:

> *Man. Because he sacrifices his health in order to make money. Then he sacrifices money to recuperate his health and he is so anxious about the future that he does not enjoy the present; the result being that he doesn't live in the present or the future; he lives as if he is never going to die, and then he dies having never lived.*

About Petra

My near-death experience taught me the magic of life, how precious each moment is and how living in the NOW is the key to happiness. There is no death, there is only transformation.
~ Petra Nicoll

Petra Nicoll is an "Emotional Energy Therapist" who helps others unravel and unveil the patterns in their individual life story, so that they can live life to their highest potential. Her easy and unique process of having clients talk through their story, enables them to clearly see how particular patterns have influenced the overall theme of their life. Their stories, like yours, are distinctive ones that have taught specific life lessons. Today, her passion and purpose is to help her clients see how these specific patterns, which create significant lessons even in the midst of much darkness, despair and grief, can become a positive influence for personal light and good.

Petra Nicoll grew up in a middle-class family in the small village of Markt Schwaben, enjoying her years of childhood innocence in a place of picturesque beauty, just fifteen miles south of Munich, the capital of Bavaria, Germany.

Petra's real life story could be fiction – only it's not. Her memoir: *Petra's Ashes "A Transcendental Story"* is thought-provoking and mesmerizing -- and perhaps even remarkable.

Sheltered and protected by her Catholic family, her story begins with life-altering changes that occurred at nine years old, during a near-death experience, which begins her lifelong journey of uncommon insights and unsettling discoveries.

The extreme pain and sorrow of her exposure to the tragic death of her mother, suicide, depression, and realities of war tell only part of Petra's story – one of a rare woman. All of her experiences lead her to the Masters of the Far East, the Shamans of North America and Mexico—through whom she awakens to the realization and vision that she has been given—to become transformed and more intuitive, authentic and soul-centered. Her extraordinary journey, and the practices and training that she has received throughout her life, has given her the tools to help others.

Petra studied psychology in London and is a Certified Life Coach. She has taught "Emotional Energy Technique" and "Traditional Usui Reiki" to over 3500 students world-wide. As an author, radio show host and public speaker, Petra has a wealth of information to share and skills to apply. Also a successful entrepreneur, she has facilitated hundreds of workshops and seminars, with proven, sustainable transformations in individuals for over thirty years.

Like a Phoenix, she will rise from the ashes of despair and soar.

Contact information:
- www.petranicoll.com
- Petra@petranicoll.com
- Tel: 541.543.9820

CHAPTER 18

WHAT'S WRITTEN IS REAL

BY STACIA PIERCE

Two very important tools that I have used time and time again to create success in my business and life: pen and paper. Writing daily in my journal changed my life from debt and disappointment to success and achievement.

I've used the principle of success journaling to plan my life and predict my future. It is one of the important success habits that I do daily. Journaling empowers me to take my ideas and turn them into reality.

WHAT'S WRITTEN IS REAL

I've always been a big dreamer. Yet there was period in my life where I was too consumed with my own tragic story to dream. My tear-stained journal was filled with frustrations, how devastated I was from a failed marriage, the struggle of being a newly-divorced single mother with no plan and no money. I wrote my sob stories in my journal daily and my life circumstances were only getting worse.

One day it dawned on me, the more I wrote about my problems, the more problems showed up in my life. It was then that I wondered what if I change the narrative and write about the life I wanted to live. I decided to use my journal as an instrument to write my own success story and predict my future.

I started listing my dreams, goals and desires. I wrote out a day in my dream life in a very detailed way. I wrote about marrying again; I wrote about building a successful business; I wrote about successfully raising my daughter and becoming very wealthy. My new narrative was a turning point in my life. At the time, I only had a small inclination that writing my dreams and goals could change my life. Within two years, I remarried, had a successful salon and store, and published my first book.

I took this simple idea of success writing and began to apply it to every area of my life. I went from just knowing success principles to powerfully activating them in my life through planning on paper.

DARE TO DREAM ON PAPER

I believe in divine appointments and connections. I believe that you gravitated to this book and are reading this chapter now because we're supposed to be divinely connected. I have written this chapter to inspire you to write a new success script for your life. To empower you to change your own narrative and use the power of journaling to write your way to success.

I am about to share with you my success writing routine. The simple and very effective writing methods that I have used in my life and in that of my clients, to manifest our greatest desires. They have not only helped me build my seven-figure empire, but have also helped many of my clients do the same.

1.   Write Affirmations

I script my life's movie with affirmations. Every month I write a new script—a picture of what's possible for my life and business. Then I meditate on it often, embodying the vision so that it becomes part of me.

When I was starting out in business and had no clients, no contracts, no cash flow, I used the power of affirmations to write my future success in present tense. Once it was written, I read it aloud daily and envisioned my big booming business.

To attract new clients, I wrote "passionate and big paying clients come to me easily and effortlessly."

Then, I spoke it, read it, visualized it, discussed it, journalized about it and one day at an event, a lady walked up to me and said how much will it cost to coach with you? I hope it is not more than five thousand dollars. I said, "that's exactly how much it costs!" She was my first coaching client and I had attracted her into my business with my affirmation.

Soon after that someone I started getting several requests from people who wanted to work with me. In only about a week, I went from zero to many clients. The words I had written worked. They manifested big success in my business and life.

I wrote several other affirmations for my business, including one that helped me confirm that I loved my business and could work as a coach long term. I wrote in my journal:

I love my business! Big business comes to me.
My business clients love me and people love paying me.

With this affirmation I built the foundation of my business, attracting new clients from around the world who loved me and wanted to work with me.

Affirmations have the power to change your circumstances very quickly. Put your desires on paper in a positive voice. Write in the present tense and as you begin to speak your affirmations, imagine yourself possessing what you're saying. The more emotions you add to it the more powerful the affirmation becomes.

2. Repetitive Writing

I practice repetitive goal writing on a daily basis so that I stay focused on what I want to achieve. A lot of people write their goals only once and never look at them again. It's impossible to achieve a goal that you're not even aware of. Every month I rewrite my 101 goals in my journal. I used to write them only once and I only accomplished a few of them. Now that I write them often, I check more and more off the list on a monthly basis.

When I was searching for my dream home, I wrote a dream home wish list with 26 very specific things I wanted in my new home. I included the square footage, a lake view, palatial landscape, gated community and so on. I made a copy of my list and gave it to my real estate agent, who at the time wasn't convinced I could have it all. Yet I was! Every morning during my time of solitude, I would rewrite my list. I did this for two weeks before the real estate agent called and excitedly shared that she had found my home. She said everything that I wanted was on the list. When I drove up to the place, I knew it was my home. I started to recognize everything that I had written on the list…it was all there!

By constantly reviewing your goals, you'll become empowered to develop an action plan to achieve them.

3.   Write Yourself Checks and Contracts.

A long time ago, I was faced with an astronomical debt that had to be paid quickly, I discovered the power of writing myself a check. I took an old checkbook and wrote myself several checks in varying amounts according to my need. I then printed my bank balance sheet and wrote in the amount of the checks plus an additional $25,000. I wanted to make sure I had a vision of my bank balance showing more than enough money to cover my need with extra money left over. I posted the checks and the bank balance sheet on a vision board that I meditated on every night.

Then I went to work in my journal, thinking, planning and writing all the ways I could manifest the money. It came to me to create a new workshop. I was able to generate all of the money I need plus some in less than 30 days!

Another client, a CEO of a company, needed $70,000 to meet payroll and other expenses. She wrote a declarative statement in her Success Journal that I created for my clients, "I have $70,000 in the bank ready to be distributed to my employees." She then added photos and positive quotes to her vision pages so that she could meditate on her desired results. Within seven days, she manifested the money needed just in time for payroll. Before using this writing routine she had never manifested money so quickly!

4.   You can command what you want to see manifest with your words.

I command my ideal circumstances and situations to manifest in my life through written statements all the time. What makes success writing so unique is the process of upgrading your mindset and channeling your positive thoughts to paper to crystalize your desires and bring about deliberate manifestation. It doesn't take a long time for what you want to appear. Once your intention is set, your desire is clear and your plan is written, what you want is delivered quickly. Command the good you want to come to pass.

I wrote a command statement to win in the Oprah's Own TV Show contest years ago. I joined the contest late, with only two weeks to go. There were thousands of entries and I really wanted to win. So, I wrote my command statement in my journal: "Millions of people would watch my video entry and vote for me." I also wrote: "Oprah would recognize me as one of the top finalists." One night I dreamt I was in 3rd place, so I added that to my statement and it manifested in a very short time exactly like I had commanded it!

Synchronicity happens when you script your life. It is God's way of guiding you into your purpose path. Writing your true desires empowers you to live beyond the limitations of the world. Everything aligns on your behalf to bring about your desired goals.

5.   Write a Gratitude list.

The most crucial step to goal manifestation is acknowledging the blessings you already have. When you take time to write out a list of things that you are grateful for, you activate a creative force to produce more blessings into your life.

In my morning meditation, I got an idea to start having my family share something good that happened for them in the previous week. As we sat at brunch, everyone seemed so challenged to sort through their week and find a positive moment to share. They could barely think of one good story, yet we kept up the exercise week after week. As time went on, everyone started having more and more things to share and were anxious to tell their stories. The exercise made us conscious of our day and the goodness that comes to us all the time. In a state of gratefulness, we all began to recognize more and more of our own blessings. The more you think about the good that happens for you, more good things that you WANT to happen for you will start to manifest.

Go through your day looking for what's right. Write a list of 50 things that you are grateful for. Read it aloud so that you can hear for yourself how good you have it.

Sometimes, it's important to express gratitude in person. While attending a fund raiser, a client walked up to a high-powered executive in her community to express gratitude for all that she had done for my client's organization. The executive was so moved, she immediately asked my client, "What can I do for you?" My client said she wanted to meet the 50 most powerful people in the city. As it turned out most of them were in the room. The executive took her by the hand and introduced her to everyone on her list, encouraging them to connect with my client's organization. That one event yielded thousands of dollars in donations and collaborations for her organization—and it all started with an expression of gratitude.

Thankfulness is the key to happiness. It builds your awareness and fosters humility as well as empowers you to continue on your success track.

Is *Success Journaling* manifestation as simple as it sounds?

Yes, it is. Success writing only works when you are real with yourself and your desires. Don't waste time writing about what you think you should desire, or what others want for you. You can only manifest your deepest desires, the ones that you are emotionally and spiritually connected to.

Once you start intentionally writing your success story and expecting results, your eyes will be opened to many opportunities and paths to help you achieve your dreams. The manifestation happens because now you have a focused plan and you are doing the inner work.

I recommend you try the success writing principles for three weeks with no days off. You'll begin to see how the Big Secret is working in your life. You'll start manifesting more income, an increase in business and a significant increase in your goals accomplished.

Begin your day with a prayer:
Heavenly Father,
I expect Miracles today…lead me to them.

About Stacia

Stacia Pierce is founder and CEO of LifeCoach2Women.com. She's affectionately known as the whole-life coach because she helps you tighten the unraveled loose ends of your life, and discover your true self so you can give one hundred percent to your career, family and personal life. After spending only a short amount of time with Stacia, you will suddenly see life from a grander, more promising perspective. She frees you to explore your creativity, embrace the possibilities of a better, more fulfilling and happier healthier way of living with her on-the-spot signature 'Success Attractions Strategies' for instant results.

Stacia's no-excuse business philosophy will empower you to take responsibility for your life and business, so you can finally live the life you've been dreaming of. She makes business easy, lucrative and fun with her vast collection of success tools, seminars and conferences for entrepreneurs. She is committed to empowering entrepreneurs around the world to live their dream life and run their dream businesses. She specializes in showing them how to turn their passion into a paycheck by creatively building an authentic business that gets them recognized for their skills and expertise, attracts their ideal clients and works for them day and night. A master of manifestation, Stacia invented the Success Journal to empower heart-centered, creative entrepreneurs to manifest their dreams and desires – using a systematic format.

CHAPTER 19

THE SUCCESS JUNGLE: GIFTS, GUIDANCE, AND BLESSINGS IN DISGUISE

BY ELIZABETH YANG

Anything is possible. Be courageous about dreaming big and always reach for the stars.

1986 was a year of change for me, despite being only three years old. My father passed away, leaving my mother all alone to raise my younger brother and myself. She'd never worked before that, and was abruptly flung into a world where she had to provide for her children and ensure their success all on her own. She was fierce in her desire to do what it took. Ultimately, the woman born in Taiwan and insisting that only Mandarin Chinese was spoken at home became "Tiger Mom."

My mother was only in her early thirties when my father passed away, but decided to focus on her children's success over finding love again. She became a Tiger Mom. For those who aren't familiar with the characteristics of this type of mother, allow me to elaborate:

A mother who puts all her energy into her chŠdren, ensuring they are culturally well-rounded, get nothing less than perfect marks in school, are well-spoken, and are "destined for success," first and foremost.

177

This was my life and I knew no other way. My acceptance of its reality was non-negotiable.

FROM THE CUB'S PERSPECTIVE

Through persistence and perspective, a great many things can be achieved.

My route to success was decided, and through discipline and precise instruction from my mother, along with an obvious amount of diligent effort from myself, I began achieving success quickly. In short, I skipped Kindergarten, made high grades, was always the teacher's pet, entered the Gifted and Talented Education (G.A.T.E) Program in 4th grade, graduated from high school early to go to Berkeley for Electrical Engineering and Computer Science (because that was what my mother told me I was going to do), and proceeded to graduate from Berkeley in just two and a half years at the age of nineteen. It was time to "get to work!"

Everything I'd achieved was impressive—quite typical of the child of a career-focused Asian American family, really—but I'd sacrificed too. I'd never been able to go to those parties in college or just relax and be myself. Everything had been so structured up to that point.

Now, my engineering career had begun at Raytheon, a government subcontractor defense company. I was surrounded by smart, passionate individuals who had chosen their careers for themselves, and while it was fascinating, it was also overwhelming. They did the same things repeatedly—day in and day out—for years. I had a great project, working on the B2 Bomber Radar Modernization Program; however, the thought of doing that for the rest of my career was decidedly unsettling. I was quite young, after all. There was only one option—go back to school to get a Master's Degree. The only problem was that I didn't want a Master's Degree in Engineering. I decided to go to law school simply to expand my knowledge of our government and legal system, so I sat for the LSATs and went to school in the evenings, working during the day. And somewhere in there, I found the time to enter into the jungle of being a "carefree" young adult for my first time ever. I loved being wild and having fun, traveling, dating, partying, and enjoying adventures.

This new life had awakened me in a most interesting way. It was absolutely contrary to what my mother had raised me to be, but I was coming into my own, recognizing that I could have these "Tiger Mom" levels of success, while embracing a more liberating life. I was out of my cage! Three and a half years later, I became an Intellectual Property (IP) Attorney, which made me feel professionally alive.

THE WORST CHALLENGES IN LIFE CAN BE INTERPRETED AS BLESSINGS IN DISGUISE

Don't wait for the thunderstorms to pass; learn to dance in the rain.

There is a book in every person and I am honored to have this opportunity to share mine. Shortly after becoming an IP attorney, I unpredictably got pregnant out of wedlock. In the Chinese culture and especially in the eyes of my mom, pregnancy before marriage was unheard of and very shameful. When I first looked at the stick with two stripes on it, I burst into tears. I did not know how to tell my mom. Eventually, I brought myself to tell her and my daughter was ultimately brought into existence. At the time, it was probably the worst situation I had ever been through, but now years later, I see that it was the best gift the universe could ever give me. Like people say, the best things in life are not planned.

After overcoming that challenge and giving birth to my son shortly thereafter, I discovered betrayal by the father of my children, the man I trusted and loved with all my heart. The pain was so deep and so strong that I did not know how to move on with my life at the time. Many of you who have had their hearts broken know what I mean. At the time, I told my friends who were supporting me that I wished I could fast forward time to six months later when my heart would at least be partially healed. Life is not so easy though, and if we want pleasure, we must be strong enough to endure the pain.

Eager to heal from the betrayal that fell upon me with no warning in my marriage, I began to study family law and conflict resolution in an attempt to finalize and resolve my own divorce. There were more days of uncertainty in my life during that time than I'd ever imagined before. At the time, it was again probably the worst situation I had ever encountered, but now that the divorce has finalized, I am able to take my family law learnings to help all those in the community who are going through child custody and child support battles. In addition to starting my own practice and expanding into family law during my divorce, I also created a chain of children's indoor playgrounds called Magical Playground, now with locations in Pasadena, West Covina and Whittier.

Without the discipline and lessons of my youth to guide my personal and professional adult life during that time, I may not have been able to figure it all out. Drastic change was needed, driven by what appeared to be bad challenges, but all directed to good outcomes based on my ability to be a go-getter in managing my life.

Today, the Law & Mediation Offices of Elizabeth Yang assist in the practice areas of Intellectual Property Law, Business Law and Family Law. In regards to IP, we assist both US-based and internationally-based clients with their legal needs in terms of patents through various partnerships for successful collaborative efforts to protect their interests abroad. In regards to business law, we assist business owners and entrepreneurs in corporate entity formation, contract drafting, business disputes and litigation. And in regards to family law, we assist families in going through possibly one of the most difficult times in life. With my mediation certification from the Los Angeles County Bar Association, I aim towards reaching a win-win resolution for both parties rather than combatively litigating through the expensive court system. Good can truly come from all experiences in life.

UNDERSTANDING PATENTS, TRADEMARKS, AND COPYRIGHTING

Ideas are a dime a dozen. So, if you have one, why not put it out there? You just never know what its fullest potential is.

Are you a hyper-protective creative visionary? It's common to be highly protective of ideas, and surely wise to protect what you feel has potential to change your life, as well as the lives of others. You must ensure you're taking effective action that gives true protection. At my law office, this is where we offer great value. Protecting you and your ideas is the focus of this part of the business.

Patents

In March of 2013, the America Invents Act (AIA) was implemented, which created a fundamental shift in how IP law was practiced. With this new law, it does not matter who invents an idea first; it matters who files the patent application first. This means you should file first, and then take care of the rest. But which patent?

There are two patent types, each with different criteria and protections.

First, there is the utility patent, which protects the functionality and use of an idea. A provisional utility patent is basic and simple, offering one year's worth of protection for a concept. It's easy to file and can be rather vague, offering the person who files it time to talk to investors, get seed money, and make decisions. If they decide it's not a good idea, they will let the patent expire. If they wish to pursue it, they can apply for a non-provisional utility patent, which offers twenty years of protection for the idea. This patent offers:

- Inventors' protections and assurance.
- The opportunity to sell ideas. Not everyone wants to run a business, some people want to invent, and with a utility patent, they have options such as exclusive rights, licensing rights, royalty income, etc.

Second, there is the design patent, which protects how something looks—for example, the appearance of an iPhone as opposed to its utility. Design patents offer fourteen years of protection.

Copyrights

Every day we can find inspiration and be awestruck by peoples' creativity and their ideas that they bring to market. Human potential is ever-amazing, and a part of what makes me love practicing IP law so much.

Copyrights are the protection of choice for writers, entertainment venues, books, poetry, music, artistic endeavors, etcetera. The copyright will protect the creator of these works, showing that they are a product of their intellectual property. Use without permission falls under plagiarism.

Trademarks

Trademarks protect names. Unlike patents, you must use a trademark in commerce. Verification that it's being used is done through submitting a specimen. This may be a picture of a storefront with the name on it, a business card, a brochure, an up-and-running website (not just a domain reservation), and an active shopping cart on the website if you sell a product or service.

The classification of goods and services is important to fully understand in trademarks, because this is linked to the trademark. For example: a shoe store can be named McDonalds and be trademarked, not interfering with the restaurant's trademark. They are different classifications with different services. The same is true for Nike—someone could open a Nike restaurant and that would not infringe on the Nike sportswear business.

A BIT ABOUT FAMILY LAW

CompassÚn-driven resolutÚns are what help
individuals to heal and move on.

My work with Family Law comes from my appreciation of how emotionally overwhelming and financially-encumbering personal life events such as divorce can create. Practicing this law fulfills a very personal part of my life, because helping people who once cared and then grew apart—whatever the reason—to become whole again is important. Not only is it important for adults to reach a resolution, but if children are involved, it affects them like a ripple effect for an entire lifetime and for generations to come. The best interests of the children are what I fight for, and knowing that divorces have a tremendous impact on their entire future, I use my personal experience to get the parents to understand that they must give up their ego for the sake of their kids.

WISDOM FOR SMART ENTREPRENEURIALISM

Set yourself up for success.

There are certain principles and strategies that I am committed to, thereby allowing me to consistently grow my vision, while simultaneously managing my current professional and personal life. This insight is what I wish to share with you:

1. Put your goals and visions in writing. If you haven't read or watched "The Secret" yet, do it. Vision boards are real and they work. Declaring "impossible" goals and dreams to the universe in writing and in detail really works as well. Put your vision board somewhere you can see every day, whether it be on your bedroom door or on your bathroom mirror and adjust each action to go towards it. Three years ago, I pulled up the vision board that I had created eight years ago and 90% of the things that I put on there had come true, including having one son and one daughter.

2. Be involved in your community and align with professional associations. Do more than donate money. Get to know people and share what you do. Spread the word. Offer your knowledge. Be of service. Give, if not money, then time. There's truth in the saying: "It's who you know, not what you know."

3. When you think you are out of ideas, there's at least a thousand more. Having an open mind and asking for support allows you to see opportunities that may otherwise be in your blind spot, offering another avenue of success.

4. Ask for support. Many folks think that asking for support is a sign of weakness but it's actually an intelligent and courageous act. Human beings were put on this planet to "be" with one another, not stand alone. Through my years of experience, I have learned one thing and that is: "I am never alone."

5. See every challenge as a blessing in disguise. Whether it be going through an ugly four-year long divorce or discovering betrayal by a trusted partner, I have always held on to this principle: "Rather than wait for thunderstorms to pass, learn to dance in the rain" and embrace all that life has to give you. Learn to make not just lemonade from lemons, but delicious lemonade.

WHY NOT PURSUE YOUR DREAMS?

Live life to the fullest; don't waste a single mŠlisecond.

As I've grown and adjusted from the daughter influenced by her "Tiger Mom" and into my own adulthood, I have learned that gratitude and appreciation is key in life. Did I always understand this? No, of course not. Most kids wouldn't. However, as a wiser person with many life experiences, I now see how all setbacks in life can be interpreted to blessings in disguise. Without going through my life challenges, I wouldn't have been able to navigate through a bitter divorce to a family law practice that helps families throughout the community.

I am the product of my mother's efforts and a woman who is keenly aware of my role in my children's lives. My actions aren't just like Mom's, exactly, but teaching my children how to have the drive to succeed, while giving them space to pursue their interests and passions is important. Life is short – so, be like water and go with the universe's flow. Accept everything; resist nothing.

About Elizabeth

Elizabeth Yang (楊安立) has been practicing law since 2007 and specializes in Intellectual Property Law, including Patent, Copyright and Trademark Prosecution and Litigation; Business Law, including corporate entity formation, contract drafting, contract disputes, litigation; Family Law, including divorce, child custody, child support, alimony, and asset division; and Traffic Citations. She is fluent in Mandarin Chinese.

Elizabeth was admitted to the United States Patent & Trademark Office in 2007. At the age of 19, she earned her Bachelor's degree in Electrical Engineering and Computer Science from UC Berkeley in two and a half years. She earned her JD/MBA from the University of La Verne. Elizabeth's IP practice is primarily focused on Intellectual Property litigation at the Federal District and before the United States Patent and Trademark Office (USPTO). Her practice also includes complex business litigation, patent prosecution and trademark prosecution.

Prior to starting the Law & Mediation Offices of Elizabeth Yang, Elizabeth gained extensive experience at various large international intellectual property law firms where her practice primarily focused on a variety of technologies, including electronics, hardware, software, variable data printers, fingerprinting sensors, data packet processing, network security systems, microprocessors, and automated telephonic systems along with IP Litigation. She is also experienced in drafting patent validity opinion letters, requests for reexamination, intellectual property licensing agreements and trademark consent agreements.

Elizabeth went through her own 4-year divorce, a blessing in disguise, because she ended up learning about all the in's and out's of the California Family Law system, personally dealing with issues involving child custody, child support, alimony, asset division, pre-nuptial agreements and post-nuptial agreements. Being a mother of two young children, she understands and can relate to clients who are also undergoing emotional divorces. She has represented Family Law clients both efficiently and compassionately at various stages of litigation and trial. Elizabeth also earned her Mediation Certification in 2015 with the Los Angeles County Bar Association (LACBA) and has assisted many combative litigants in resolving their issues through mediation and alternate dispute resolution.

Elizabeth also started a chain of children's indoor playgrounds called Magical Playground, now with locations in Pasadena, West Covina and Whittier. It offers a safe, clean and fun place for parents and caregivers to bring their kids to enjoy hands-on play time as well as providing a venue to host birthday parties.

Prior to practicing law, Elizabeth worked for Raytheon Company as an electrical engineer designing radar systems for the B2 Bomber. She has also interned at the NASA Jet Propulsion Lab, working as a team member on the main control unit of the Mars Exploration Rover. Elizabeth has been awarded a "Rising Star" by Super Lawyers, as well as "Top 100 Civil Lawyers" and "Top 40 Lawyers Under 40" by the National Trial Lawyers Association.

Elizabeth resides in Los Angeles with her husband Phil and her two children, Liliana and Alexander. She enjoys playing poker, salsa dancing, traveling, and being a foodie in her spare time.

CHAPTER 20

DREAM BIG
THE UNIVERSE IS LISTENING

BY ILONA SELKE

Have you ever manifested a parking spot when you needed one? Many people have had some success with manifesting at least some things. Yet there remain questions about how to manifest effectively, why it can happen and how it works. Today I want to take you on a journey into discovering an even bigger secret.

To find out just how big the secret is, join me on a journey to Hawaii in a moment! But first let me summarize how far we have come in our understanding of the universe so far.

The book and movie *The Secret* has rekindled the desire to understand the hidden and ancient laws of the universe. These ancient laws reveal that we are not just physical bodies, nor mere cogs in the wheel of life. However, during the last 800 years and especially in the era of *Enlightenment*, human kind has been obsessed with discovering repeatable laws of nature and rather pursued the scientific understanding of the universe, which brought us the body-mind split.

In our modern age, this has brought us space travel and the internet. We have externalized our thinking abilities and created a huge empire of 'things.' Many thought leaders now seriously consider that the mind is the equivalent of consciousness and that it maybe be transferrable into a computer.

The *Transhumanist* movement is trying to suggest the use of sophisticated technologies to greatly enhance human intellectual, physical, and psychological capacities, opening the doors to the creation of cyborgs. Even Elan Musk, the inventor of the TESLA CAR and co-founder of PayPal and Space X, believes it is our only chance to survive the advent of AI (Artificial Intelligence). They promote the creation of an **Übermensch**, a world where God is dead and the Soul is but an aspect of the body. AI, cyborgs and robots are the epitome of this kind of thinking.

And yet, you and I are here because we have discovered that there is a very different kind of universe afoot. We can affect change in the matrix of time-space through our focused attention, *The Secret* says.

Many of us are slowly discovering the deeper nature of the universe and Quantum Physicists are puzzled. It is likely that you are part of this movement of pioneers that is on the brink of discovering the bigger secrets of the universe.

Let us start with religions. All religions have in common that they teach us that we can talk to God, the universe, or various deities. They teach that our thoughts can have effect. The fact that our prayers are answered and that we can witness magical results down here on Earth due to our conscious focus, is in itself a mind-boggling feat. Think about it! It implies that we are truly living in a dreaming matrix rather than a solid state universe. We are indeed living in a consciousness-interactive universe, as plenty of miracles stories from all over the world prove to us.

Just how do you and I take part in this discovery of this greater universe? And what is *THE BIG SECRET?* Join me now on the journey to Hawaii.

My husband and I lived on the Big Island of Hawaii for a good part of 12 years – doing research with wild dolphins, about their telepathic and other extraordinary healing effects. I chronicled these amazing encounters and lessons I learned from the dolphins in two of my books, called *WISDOM OF THE DOLPHINS* and *DOLPHINS, LOVE and DESTINY.*

On this day, Don and I were driving back 'Home' from the airport, ready to be back into the swing of our island life on Hawaii. We had been gone for over four months, being on a seminar tour through Europe. Close to our house, just a few streets away, was a dolphin beach where dolphins frequently came into a little-known bay.

Just as we turned onto our road which was bordering onto a National Forest Reserve, we had to face a shocking view: Three abandoned cars that had been dropped off onto our street and had turned our paradise into a junk yard in our absence.

As we got out of our car, our nearly toothless neighbor greeted us. In her scratchy voice, she bemoaned, "I have called the cops, the city, everyone, over and over for the last three months to come pick up these Junkers but no results. They just don't care." The state of Hawaii was, in fact, known for not bothering to clean all the streets, especially in the more rural areas, and many old relics of junk cars had already remained on the roadside for decades.

Today I was not taking NO for an answer. There had to be a way to have my paradise back. My emotions were upset and I was not happy. However, I firmly believed by now that all possibilities exist simultaneously, as Hugh Everett and Wheeler postulated in their interpretation of Quantum Physics, saying that *'many parallel realities exist simultaneously.'*

Also Brian Greene has postulated in the Super String Theory that there are extra dimensions of space-time. The new scientific thinking is indeed pointing to a reality that is far beyond the atomic model that has dominated our minds until now. **Science is starting to meet magic.** Quantum Physics has proven in experiments [EPR Experiment, etc.] that our consciousness or our focused attention is part and parcel of crafting the outcome, at least at the microcosmic level.

I had already experienced that a change in myself could create a change in the macrocosm that surrounds me, if I simply tune into the universe of my choice and dip the cup of my awareness into the ocean of the many parallel choices.

Looking at the junk cars, I instantly wondered if there was anything that I had done wrong. Before approaching the universe with a request for a bigger miracle, we need to have a *positive balance* on our *Karmic Credit Card.* This may or may not be news to you, but a clear conscience is a prerequisite for an extraordinary and magical life.

Don and I took our luggage into our house and as quickly as I could, I arranged my little meditation room and lit a candle. After having calmed my mind and body, I started by dropping my brainwave state down into the Alpha and Theta levels, which are around 4 – 8 Hz. This is the mindset that is usually associated with meditation. However, this is only the launching pad for reaching even greater awareness states.

As I entered a clearer, calmer state of mind, I started pulling up into higher Gamma brainwaves, (22 Hz to 100 Hz, but usually centering on 40+ Hz).

Research in gamma-band oscŠlatÚns may explain the heightened sense of conscÚusness, bliss and intellectual acuity subsequent to meditatÚn.
~ Wikipedia.

That day, I simply imagined that I was raising my innermost core of awareness, my soul, to the highest point in the universe. This has the side effect of raising our brainwave frequency into the Gamma range. I aimed at entering the point of singularity. This is where I feel God and I are one. Some people say they imagine being a rocket or a beam of light that flies and unites with the center of creation.

Once I was in that pristine state of heightened stillness, I nearly forgot my deepest wish of that day. But I pulled all my awareness together and remembered that I was on a mission and wanted to land my rocket ship in a parallel universe, one in which the street was returned to my Heaven on Earth. Despite the outer negative circumstances, I re-focused on the end-result that I really wanted while in this *singularity state*. I could liken this shifting to rearranging the matrix around me until it fit my sense of alignment.

Requests for larger miracles that deeply matter to us have the fuel needed to shift the blueprint of life. The request will have the required energy to enter the eye of the needle and to come out on the other side of the looking glass, allowing you to appear in the parallel world of your choice.

In this heightened state of awareness, while being deeply relaxed and focused into oneness, I witnessed the return of my Paradise in my inner vision. I imagined that I was entering the hologram of my pristine *Heaven on Earth*, complete with a clean street. I had once read somewhere that at moments of 100% certainty, a supernatural feeling sets in. This lets people know that they are completely on target. I entered into this reverie until I had that 100% feeling of certainty.

When my inner image of my desired future really hit the perfect resonant spot in the cosmos, it indicated to me that my vision of my perfect future was about to manifest. This inner certainty is far different from going out on a limb of faith, and buying things on a credit card with the firm assumption that the money will follow, which people commonly do.

A precise alignment is needed for the perfect outcome to manifest in the external world. We have to know, for sure, when we have arrived at the right portal of the parallel dimension of our choice. Indeed, we need to know when we have reached the time-space that holds the fulfilment of our dream.

When we set the dial of time-space onto the desired coordinates, we do this in our body, mind and soul. Our entire self is vibrating to a higher tune at that moment. Actually, we already do this with every single thought and feeling every minute of the day, albeit often unconsciously, or with expectations that are shaped by our culture.

However, the more you and I are awakened to this co-creative process of becoming a conscious dreamer, the better the outcomes. When we awaken to the fact that we are dreaming, we are increasingly free to live the life of our dream.

We have to set our focus on a desired outcome and notice when the resonance peak with the 'universe' has been reached. When we are more experienced, life will flow more and more gracefully and our mere thoughts will unfold as perfect creations before us, removing even the need to create any changes.

While still sitting in my meditation room in Hawaii, I suddenly heard some crunchy metallic sounds. "Could that be trucks coming to pick up those cars already?" I marveled. I thought to myself, "Better not check and simply keep meditating." As the saying goes: *A watched pot never boils*. We need to let go and let God. "After all, at the end of our short street, a house was being built using a crane and it might just be the workers there creating the crunchy sounds," I reasoned.

After finishing my meditation, Don and I drove to our little Hippie town called *Pahoa* to have dinner, as our refrigerator and stomachs both were empty. I totally forgot to check up on my experiment as we drove out onto our street. BUT, on our way back home that night, I made sure to check on my reality. Had it shifted as the sounds had almost indicated to me, or not? SUCCESS! Our street was again back to its perfect state of pristine perfection, and my paradise was back in order.

Initially, I questioned the miracle and did what most readers might be doing right now: I wondered if this miracle was a mere coincidence and I briefly looked for a logical answer.

But then I quickly recalled the many other miracles which I had already experienced. I remembered my lesson from long ago: *Logic wants to have a neat and orderly progression of cause and effect. However, miracles don't happen in a logical sequence.* **Miracles depend on our ability to lift ourselves outside of the ordinary logical time-space sequence.**

Logic is the basis of our scientific world view and has its place. However, the BIG SECRET is that we don't live in a solid world nor a solid reality. We manifest those circumstances that are in keeping with our beliefs and our vibrational state. Once you learn that you are the creator of your life, you will have liberties and abilities that far surpass the normal laws of physics.

In the beginning, learning to manifest is about *mastering your ability to focus* and *raising your vibration*. It is about learning that your *conscious and subconscious mind affect your reality.*

When you master that, you will realize that *life is a living hologram.* You then become the conscious time-space co-creator and director of your life. The frequency of your soul will be reflected in what you manifest around you. We live in a Multiverse, and you live in your version of Heaven on Earth.

Happiness and feelings of bliss will let you know when you are on the right path. Pain, unhappiness and even suffering will let you know when you are out of phase with life. We all want to manifest a better life with more money, greater health, and a soulmate. And YES, this is all possible.

However please remember: Life is not about manifesting 'things.' *Our increased manifestation skills are a side effect of raising our vibration.* That is what evolution is all about. Shining greater light and more love is the real purpose of our life. As you evolve, the world around you will reflect more love and light back to you.

STOP – LOOK – AND CHOOSE

Any moment of life you can step out of the film that you are currently living in and become aware that you are the director. *You can refocus on what you really want.* You sit in the director's chair of your life. Increased bliss and happiness will be your rewards.

Remember: ***Dare to dream big, the Universe is listening!***

About Ilona

Ilona Selke is an international author and seminar leader, lecturer, and musician. She has written four books and has 25 CDs to her name, and has been quoted in numerous books for her work. Her books and teachings have been translated into English, German, French, Spanish, Chinese, Russian, Polish, Czechoslovakian and Hindi. Her new book, *DREAM BIG – The Universe Is Listening* will be published in June 2017.

Since 1987, Ilona Selke has been teaching personal growth seminars in Europe, Americas and Asia – to therapists, teachers, doctors, business people and laymen alike.

During the last 30 years, Ilona Selke has inspired thousands of people worldwide to discover the power of their consciousness and how to create a successful life.

She has appeared on TV and on Radio, on the well-known *Hay-House Summit* in English and German, and has appeared as an inspirational speaker on many telesummits. She has also been a favorite speaker at many conferences, such as the *Prophet's Conferences*, the Q*uantum Energy Conferences*, the *Global Sciences*, and the *Global Spiritual Scientist*, etc.

Ilona Selke and her husband Don Paris, Ph.D., are co-founders and directors of Living From Vision®, a company committed to teaching about the holographic nature of the universe and how human consciousness can intentionally interact with the 3-Dimensional world.

The Living From Vision® course, available online or in book form, teaches methods of goal setting, creating success and manifestation skills through a holographic whole-brain method. The LFV course has been translated into six languages and has been taught worldwide through a network of LFV Teachers and Coaches since 1990.

Additionally, Ilona Selke and her husband have been involved in the research of a quantum tool called the SE-51000 since 1987, for which her husband received an honorary Ph.D. in 2000.

In 2007, they built the inspiring *Shambala Oceanside Retreat Center* on the Northshore of Bali; as well as a Wellness Spa called *Shambala Spa* in Ubud, the heart of Bali with a total of 30 employees in Bali, which they still run to this date.

From 2004 – 2014 Ilona Selke and her husband owned a *Dolphin Watch* boat in Key

West, where they still offer Wild Dolphin Encounters. Numerous articles and Ilona Selke's books chronicle the astounding research and discoveries she made with the dolphins in her over 1000 hours of underwater contact with wild dolphins.

Ilona Selke has her own TV show called *Quantum Living* on WBTVN every Sunday at 8 PM CST. Replays can be found on www.quantumliving.guru

Ilona Selke and her husband divide their time between their home in Bali and their home on an island in the Pacific Northwest in the U.S.A.
- Email: info@ilonaselke.com

WEBLINKS
- www.livingfromvision.com
- www.quantumliving.guru
- www.baliseminars.com
- www.lebenausdervision.com
- www.se-5.com
- www.ubudmassage.com
- www.chiorganizer.com

- FB: www.facebook.com/ilona.selke

- TWITTER: IlonaSelke

CHAPTER 21

THE THRIVING LIFE

BY ALLISON D'ANNA

At 20, I was diagnosed with autoimmune hepatitis. I would wake up and take handfuls of prescription drugs each day – everything from steroids to anti-inflammatories. As a result of years of drugs my weight blew up, my skin broke out, and I was left with digestive, weight, and hormonal issues. At the time, my life was like a roller coaster and I experienced so many different emotions on a daily basis. I suffered from anxiousness, moodiness, and frequently overreacted. I was in and out of combative relationships. I craved drama to help me escape from what was going on inside. I was responding to life and striving for the next high. **I was constantly looking outside to fulfill that deep inner void I felt bubbling deep inside me. I was craving the attention outside to fulfill the lack of self-love that I felt inside.**

I had hit rock bottom to the point where I could no longer get out of bed in the morning because I felt like I had no purpose or anything propelling me to start the day. I attended a one day seminar and it left me questioning about my life. That night I went to bed filled with tears, which was the same as most nights. This night, in particular, I went to bed asking this question. . . **Is this really all there is to life? . . . Is this it?**

The next morning, I woke up and sprung from my bed searching for a piece of paper and wrote this down: *I am in charge of my happiness, my health, MY LIFE.* **This is when my life took a drastic shift.** What I began to realize was that the people that had loved their lives *had taken* *action to co-create the life they dreamed up*, they weren't just lucky or stumbled into a great life.

I started to really think about what I truly wanted for my life. For one, I knew I wanted a loving, supportive relationship. I chose to made the choice to get clear about exactly what that would look like. I got a pen and paper, and I filled the paper on both the back and front with all the characteristics I wanted in a man and a relationship. **I focused on this paper daily.** I carried it around with me in my purse and when I felt down I read it. Six months later, I was shopping at Whole Foods Grocery store, and in the checkout line, I met the man of my dreams. **He met every characteristic of my sheet of paper and even down to the way he looked at me.**

Now, I thought, could this have been a coincidence or did I manifest what I had been looking for in a relationship all along?

So, why am I telling you about this? Well, what this all comes down to, is about how my journey led to my passion for sharing my belief about how happiness is not only achieved by focusing on one aspect of life, but by **focusing on the whole picture**. What I have found is that when I focused on one aspect of my life such as health, it wasn't necessarily making me happy. **It wasn't until I realized that I needed to focus on all aspects of my life, and really get clear about what I want that I found happiness within myself.** This approach significantly changed my life, and helped me gain tremendous clarity. I am excited to share with you how it can change your life as well.

SELF-CARE

The tool that I want to share with you focuses on having **self-care at the center of everything** that you are working towards. I look at this like a flower, and self-care is at the center, surrounded by all other aspects of life. **Just like with my story, without properly taking care of myself, nothing else was working, and nothing else was going to fall into place for me. Self-care is also at the center of the flower because if you don't nurture and take care of your body or life, you will not have enough energy, or life force, to get through this journey.** Taking care of yourself is one of the most difficult jobs. It requires you put time into developing yourself and getting more satisfied with yourself and your life – listening to your inner voice nudging you in the next direction.

Self-love is getting to the higher expression of yourself. Love is being and showing your openness, vulnerability, and rawness to expand. It's facing your darkest parts of yourself and experiencing your ecstasy and happiness, **shedding layers of ourselves that no longer serve us, healing painful memories and being a better version than we were yesterday.**

CAREER AND JOURNEY

The next petal and aspect of **creating happiness focuses on career and journey**, and I have a very personal story to share with you in regards to my journey with my career, and finding what it truly was I desired to do. It all started when I had a friend who got me a job selling timeshare, and although this is quite different than what I do now, it's an important piece to my journey. When I showed up to the job, I was given 30 days of training and then was let loose to sell a $30,000 timeshare in 90 minutes. I remember saying, to my friend all these people are just here for the discount Disney tickets, none of them are interested in buying a timeshare. She said, Duh! That is why they hired you. That is your job to convince them in 90 minutes that they need this.

This brought a new challenge my way. I had never sold anything. To keep this job, I had to perform or they would let me go within 30 days. I felt the heat from the fire and this burning desire to be successful, not only financially but to show myself I could do it. I looked to my previous experience and got clear about exactly what I wanted. I wanted to be in the top 10 salespeople at the resort. I decided to go to the top salesman at the resort. His name was Brad, and he was considered a god at the resort. He sold pretty much every tour he took out. It seemed to me like magic. I asked him to mentor me and take me under his wing and show me his magic.

I spend hours going on tour with him and studying his behavior, and he spent hours going on tour with me studying my behavior and ways I could improve. He told me to record my presentation in the days I was selling so I could break it down and study it. In 90 days, I went from '0' sales to the top saleswoman at the resort, and I was invited to sell in Cabo San Lucas, Mexico. I was making so much money, and I felt like I was on top of the world, until I arrived in Mexico at the resort. The manager had put me and another woman only doing half the tour and having another come in at the end and close our deals. The men that all travelled to Mexico with all encouraged me – close my own deals! Why are you having someone come in and close your deals when you were doing them all by yourself there. I wasn't selling and the next six months turned into a sentence. What I see now was that **I didn't have the belief and support from outside anymore.** My career as a timeshare saleswoman came to a halt and **drove me to the belief I had failed which fueled me to look deeper into what I really wanted for my life.**

I have now come to the point where I enjoy the journey wherever I am. I have found in my own journey there are failures, twists, and u-turns. I just made a decision to keep moving forward. I have seen that there will always be the next shiny object to achieve, but for ultimate fulfillment, we enjoy the here and now.

I am now in my first job back at work after having my children. **This is the first experience that I am creating from a place of a soul calling.** I am not dependent on an employer or working just any old job. I started a health and wellness blog. I'm in the process of publishing a cookbook and spreading the message of health and wellness to thousands of people.

WISDOM

Wisdom is another key component to achieving that journey you desire. One of my biggest lessons was to start trusting my own wisdom and understanding of what feels right for me—to start listening to my intuition and gut to be able to make the highest decision for me. This meant being more aware of my thoughts and feelings and effortlessly expressing them.

We are in a **culture with information overload**. It's time to shut off the constant bombardment of the brain with facts and start seeking wisdom. Wisdom is the ability to discern or judge what is true, right or lasting. **Wisdom demands that you don't just listen like sheep** and accept everything you hear. Reaching for wisdom for me meant that I needed to start listening to my intuition and make the best decision for myself, and that was to pursue my dreams, and attend the Institute for Integrative Nutrition, and to practice and teach yoga.

I decided to stop watching TV and decided to **guard my mind with what I was filling it with.** This path led me to practice and then teach yoga and to attend The Institute for Integrative Nutrition. Through this journey, I developed a deeper sense of spirituality which **overflowed into all aspects of my life**. I started to create healthy and more conscious habits to eat better, and to figure out ways to communicate more effectively.

I reorganized my life to start doing things that **fed my soul and made me feel good from the inside out**. My perspective shifted to a place of empowerment. What could others do for me to what could I do to serve others? From this perspective, anything was possible because a new world opened up for me.

THE JOURNEY

I am now enjoying the journey. **Though the journey is still filled with struggles, sacrifice, and days of feeling off, the difference now is that I am asking myself better questions,** taking action when I feel frustrated and not living in that state of negativity. I now have a feeling of more in control of my life and destiny.

I had to change my perspective and realized **I had fears of failing, comparison, and judgment, but I was not going to let it stop me from making and living the life I want. I had a hunger driving me from a deeper place** and pulled me forward despite all the circumstances. I realized that without failure, I can't succeed and I can't have a voice without risk of criticism, I can't love without the risk of loss. I had fears but they weren't going to stop me from moving forward. **I had to believe in myself and start trusting myself and my own ideas. To stop looking outside for the answers.**

I realized the stronger I became the larger the voices of criticism came but I set up processes and systems that set me up to be more successful. Creating habits and routines that made it easier than recreating the wheel every day.

I had to redefine what success meant to me. I felt like I was programmed by society to believe success was something different. **Once I achieved what society said was successful, I thought there has to be something more. I then realized success is an ongoing journey.**

One of the most transformational aspects of my journey was realizing that all of this has no meaning unless I had **true self-love—which would give me a deeper sense of self-worth and confidence in myself so I could feel more confident and comfortable in my own skin.** It helped me accept others and be more open and receptive to them. It also helped me to see when others would be critical of me not to internalize this, but to receive it and see if it was mine or their projection of themselves onto me.

I realized that no true success or anything else can come before self-love. I realized that if I didn't have self-love everything I would be doing would be toward fill that void. **I realized I could change my clothing, address and spouse, but the same would perpetuate in my life again because nothing changed inside. It was merely changing outside.**

I started **focusing on the things I could control, my emotions, the meanings I gave events and most importantly, my focus.** I was living a life pending on other people's ideas, thoughts and emotions and made myself a chameleon to be liked and loved. In the end, it only created more resentment and a feeling of helplessness. I was angry at other people for my having to change rather than seeing it was I who made that choice.

Today I take risks, do what makes me uncomfortable, trust in my own ideas, and love myself more and more each day. It's a journey filled with spills, falls, failures, joy, love, and happiness and I embrace it as it comes. My hope is that you embrace your journey, and that at the center of it all you focus on self-care, and self-love.

Ask yourself, are you embracing your journey?

About Allison

When I was 20, I was diagnosed with "Autoimmune hepatitis." Essentially, this means that while I was trying to eat, live and enjoy my youth, my immune system had other ideas. I stayed on steroids and anti-inflammatories for four years. I had digestive problems, acne, unwanted weight gain and a myriad of other health issues.

About 14 years ago, I made the choice to stop eating processed foods and only consume ingredients I could pronounce. I went on a journey to search for more ways to nourish my wellbeing, which led me to attend the Institute for Integrative Nutrition and become certified in yoga.

There are so many aspects of life that contribute to our wellness. The most obvious of them, food, is only a small part of the many factors that create our sense of fulfillment. Whether it be exercise, spirituality, career choices, love, or family, there are a huge number of choices we make each day that determine who we are and how we feel.

I believe wellness is a choice. Since choosing to lead a well and balanced life, I've witnessed a total shift in not only my physical form, but also in my overall happiness.

For more information on a living a thriving life, visit:
- http://ignitingwellness.com/

CHAPTER 22

"THAT WITHIN"

BY DR. JESSICA L. VERA

What do you believe is your greatest asset? What sets you apart from the other billions of souls on this planet? What is the big secret that is intentionally pursued by many because it propels them to a life of fulfillment and abundance? These are questions of SIGNIFICANCE.

The answer is found in the examination of your uniqueness. Each of us, no matter our genetic origin, cannot be replicated. Not even identical twins are genetically identical. Why? It's because of "that within."

That within, is your ESSENCE and without it, you would not exist.

Since the turn of the century we have identified aw-ha-phenomena that we have been unable to empirically substantiate and yet we know them to be real. Science has unlocked and explained some of the mysteries of how we physiologically function but there are still things that cannot be tested, touched, or consciously identified that make you who you are.

Contributors to Science and Human Philosophy such as Buckminster Fuller, Napoleon Hill, and Jim Rohn; and psychologists Carl Jung, Lev Vygotsky, and Richard Davidson (who influenced the collective unconscious of Baby Boomers, Gen X and Millennials reaching actualizing-maturity), gave us conceptual constructs of universal laws predicated upon suppositions of how and why the universe, and we within it, operate optimally. Energy and flow, vibration and resonance all being concepts of relevance to this paradigm of thinking.

However, unsurprisingly, despite our greatest centurial contributions to raising the consciousness of humanity, our attempts to go behind the veil have led to a paradox. The more we believe we are affecting awareness, the less we collectively evolve socially. Humanity remains plagued by man-made dissonance and psychopathology, disparity, depravity, and exploitation, which has been evident since the emergence of man.

What are we missing?

The first writings of God, the Creator of our universe, emerged in the Middle Ages, and the Bible has been the number one bestseller book - for the written Word throughout the last 2,000+ years. Man has made attempts to deconstruct its existence in various ways through human-developed disciplines, but no consensus has been reached, and this disparity has led to much discord and debate.

Over the last century, universal laws, best practices, and New Age thought leaders have proposed and adapted information to provide mental constructs that substantiate experience of the unseen. Yet still there are those who, despite experiencing miracles, refuse to believe and more importantly, to act in ways that work and promote the good of all humanity.

But those in gratitude to the contributions of the pragmatists of our century, now have become more attentive to igniting and evolving our essence rather than just theorizing and testing principles. From this paradigm of thinking, a shift has started from one of externalized meaning to one of finding meaning from within first.

As an experienced trauma-graduate, life learner, humanist, and practical change agent, my reading has led to the identification of various adaptations, excerpts, and repositioning of thought, but "that within" transcends all human knowledge. It cannot be tangibly explained in words alone. It is an experienced relational congruence that begins from within and connects your essence to the Universe.

In the last several years, increased awareness of the significance of the mind-body-soul connection and its interdependent relationship has led to an increasing use of ancient practices to ignite, sustain, and to promote "that within." Mindfulness meditation is one of the practices that offers tools that work to enhance intentional awareness. The key to mindfulness is a non-judgmental awareness that enables you to respond with greater clarity, stability and understanding to life stressors, rather than reacting in unhealthy ways.

Mindfulness practice means maintaining a moment-by-moment awareness of your thoughts, feelings, bodily sensations, and surrounding environment. It involves acceptance – meaning that we pay attention to thoughts and feelings without judging them...without believing that there's a "right" or "wrong" way to think or feel in a given moment. When we practice mindfulness, thoughts tune into what we're sensing in the present moment rather than rehashing the past or imagining the future.

Though it has its roots in Buddhist meditation, secular practice of mindfulness entered the American mainstream – in part through the work of Jon Kabat-Zinn and his Mindfulness-Based Stress Reduction (MBSR, 1979). Since then, thousands of studies have documented the physical and mental health benefits of mindfulness in general, and stress reduction in particular. The far-reaching implication is the development of compassion, enhanced learning and longevity of life through the core practice of 'intention, attention, and attitude' mindful meditation (Shapiro, S).

Bodies of research are attempting to substantiate integration of informed techniques and strategies from ancient practices to promote trust, compassion, and empathy, and to eliminate blocks that impede alignment – both through therapeutic relationships and self-healing.

Through my one-on-one work with thousands seeking to maximize their life's potential, I developed a 3-Step Process Model that promotes one's ability to "Reset, Realign, and Reconcile" faulty beliefs, feelings and behavior that stifle growth due to unconscious mind-blocks. The Process Model is predicated on autobiographical and empirical data, and three decades of clinical experience. Through this Process Model, you can efficiently reprogram neuropathways previously hampered by cognitive emotive dissonance. You see, all of us have lived through adversities. However, depending upon when they occurred, (most impactful if they occurred in childhood), and the emotion associated with the experience, faulty beliefs were imprinted in the subconscious. As a result, our behavior is predisposed in ways predominately unconscious, and it is these reactive behaviors that in turn, can compromise emotional intelligence and potential.

The good news is that you have control to Change Your Mind. Change Your Life.™

Let me share the quick 3-R Process Model.

The first R, *Reset*, involves identifying triggers laden in emotion and rationalizing them to change their impact on your thoughts. This step significantly enhances Emotional Intelligence (EI) because it optimizes the ability to monitor your own and other's feelings and emotions, to discriminate among them and to use this information to guide thinking and actions (Salovey and Mayer, 1990). When you are able to clear and break through faulty beliefs/mindset blocks, then your EI becomes a conduit for elevated consciousness and intuitive flow.

Intuitiveness is the essential tenet of a success mindset, and it correlates typically with imagination and creativity – two assets most valuable to achieve what you desire.

The second R, *Realign*. Once you're ready to take responsibility for your own well-being and wholeness, opening yourself up to deprogram blocks using neuro-linguistic and energy psychology strategies, faulty beliefs and thoughts can release negativity and increase vibration daily to attract opportunities, people and resources. Life-affirming-based language is an essential ingredient. This step requires intentional action to eliminate blocks in order to reclaim your power position in all areas of life.

One technique offered by energy psychology built upon the ancient Chinese Medicine practice of working through identified energy meridians. Thought Field Therapy (TFT) also known as Meridian Tapping (Craig, G. [1990] and Carrington, P.) revolutionized therapeutic work to eradicate FEAR and it coined the phrase, "The One Minute Wonder." By tapping on all meridian points, while simultaneously using positive affirming language that focuses on the specific fear, anxiety, or phobia, emotional problems have been almost instantaneously eliminated. This technique, which is self-guided, can be used in my process step of realignment.

The 3rd R, *Reconcile*, addresses the essential absolutes needed to ignite "that within." The key here is that your essence, once evolved, then becomes aligned to the Universe. It first requires an openness amidst dissonance in order to permit internal reconciliation. Shame, Guilt and harbored Anger must be eradicated, so that Gratitude, Forgiveness and Love emanate in their place.

Within my process, knowing that you are a unique creation in progress is central, and should not be confused with motivation towards perfection. Perfection is not attainable because it is not real. Therefore, no matter where you find yourself on the continuum hierarchy of self-awareness, the focus on Self-Love first through the surrender of past history, and a focus on character strengths is indispensable to effect a reconciliation and alignment between your essence and the Universe.

Empirical findings have substantiated physiological aspects of enhanced brain function from practicing mindfulness (it increases the release of Oxytocin [happy hormone] while simultaneously decreasing Cortisol [stress hormone]) and Meridian Tapping (eradicates negative emotion through an understanding of kinetic energy release that can be measured). These and other therapeutic techniques and strategies are used to address cognitive emotive dissonance and to effect change. Once change begins, it positions you to become open to a relational congruence with the Universe.

This relational congruence relies on a highly-resonating feeling of Faith. Through Faith, we accept other intangibles that cannot be scientifically explained based upon favorable external reinforcement such as money and influence. And some of us even recognize that Faith is the most powerful positive energy.

The heart, soul, and mind (intangible constructs like air) envelop your core essence, therefore reconciliation to the Universe can only occur with acceptance of unconditional Supreme Love. When you let this light into your essence it releases limitless potential.

The latter requires you to 'step out of your own way.' Logic becomes illogical and Self-Love fuels the power principle. Self-Love is not to be confused with Love of Self – a belief that is being proliferated by egocentric thinkers.

You might be thinking it sounds simple, this Self-Love, but become aware, if you experienced unsolicited and difficult-to-explain events between the ages of 4 or 5 through 8 or 9, it can present a substantial, and at times stifling, challenge. These adversities imprint in the subconscious and create dissonance between your now self and your potential self. These circumstances create a need at times for a deeper-dive. Think of it like peeling an onion. Each layer that is eliminated, the closer you are to releasing your core powerhouse.

As you make progress, the varying adversities, set-backs in life, provide clues to the unique passion-work that you were created to share with the world. Once realized and cleared, mind-blocks no longer stifle your growth and potential, because now in awareness, you are fully present and charged-up. Your set-back becomes your set-up to level-up through resilience.

Resilience affects adaptation despite significant life adversity. It is a phenomenon – a hypothetical construct that is inferred from your manifested competent functioning despite experiencing significant adversity. Resilience is a learned protective capacity. It allows you to set-up into success.

At the heart of resilience is belief in oneself—but also belief in something larger than oneself. The resilient maintain self-esteem despite the powerful influence of others. They refrain from blaming themselves and choose to only externalize blame, but internalize success. They take responsibility for what goes right in their lives and choose to positively position themselves by cultivating opportunities.

Here is a simple self-guided linguistic strategy you can use to cultivate resilience. Take five minutes and think along three lines of affirming language (adapted, Edith Grotberg, Ph.D.):

1. **I Have:** strong relationships, structure, rules at home, and role models—these are external supports that are provided.
2. **I Am:** a person who has hope and *faith*, cares about others, and I am proud of myself— these are inner strengths that can be developed.
3. **I Can:** communicate, solve problems, gauge the temperament of others, and seek good relationships—these are all interpersonal and problem-solving skills that are acquired.

When the Universal Light, which is unconditional, is accepted, all energy can be focused on Trust of fulfillment of Divine promises. Joy is connected to your uniqueness of purpose and the promise of its perfect completion. Through mind-block clearing, neurocognitive reprogramming, strength building, and the practice of Love, Compassion, and Gratitude, your ebbs and flow in life take on new meaning. You become unstoppable and attract all that you desire and beyond. There are no limits.

Especially for you, I am sharing the Seven (7) Core Success Principles that succinctly provide the framework of your ESSENSE:

1) **E**xist – purposefully
2) **S**oul – power
3) **S**ense – emotional intelligence
4) **E**manate – positive synergistic energy
5) **N**avigate – ebbs and flows with resilience
6) **C**haracter – strengths
7) **E**ssential – absolutes

When you master these seven core success principles, then your essence – "that within," is aligned to the Universe and this intimate relationship creates a synergistic energy flow. Outer negativity does not impact inner Self-Love. Accelerated Success becomes increasingly probable due to your emanating positive synergistic energy that attracts exactly what you need. It is this relational congruence that explains those miraculous encounters, opportunities and resources that present themselves at just the right moment in time – typically far exceeding anything that you could have planned yourself.

However, when dissonance is allowed to continue, Self-Love is vulnerable and permeable. The influence of others' expectations, value judgements, and negative criticism become imprinted, and detrimentally affect your ability to claim your abundance. Under these conditions, FEAR (a powerful, negatively-charged emotion) prevails and repels desires, blocks intuition and imagination. Creativity is overpowered by unequivocal inaction.

Do you want an abundant-fulfilled life? Then ignite your ESSENCE with the Universal Light and do the clearing and reprogramming work needed. Practice Compassion, Love, and Gratitude. Leverage your intuitive imagination to create significance that is unique to you; and flood the world with your gifts in service to others for the good of all humanity. In the process, you will be enriched beyond your dreams.

About Dr. J

Dr. J., a Professional Success Coach, Entrepreneur, Best-Selling Author, Mentor, Forensic Expert and Clinician has built a real-life platform from her personal journey through trauma to victory, and founded three multi-million dollar corporations in the process. In her early twenties, she was named Latin Female Entrepreneur of the Year and became known in business as the Millionaire-Made Entrepreneur™. Her philosophy of 'collaborative leveraging for the betterment of the world' leads one of her heart-passions to empower and to promote other emerging and re-emerging socially-conscious entrepreneurs through pragmatic strategic mentoring and capitalization. Dr. J., selected as one of America's PremierExperts™, has been featured on NBC, ABC, and CBS television affiliates speaking on Neurocognitive and Neurolinguistics' Reprogramming from Trauma to Success, The Power of Self-Love, Resilience (turning life's adversities [setbacks] into one's greatest setups for leveling up), Igniting One's Core Powerhouse, and Integrated Energy Neuro-Scientific Ancient Healing Practices, and Vocational Diversification and Asset Building by leveraging the Power of the Internet.

She earned her Doctoral Degree from Barry University and holds numerous specialization certifications and licensures in areas of expertise. Over the last three decades, Dr.J. has dedicated her life's-work to personally empowering and equipping thousands to reach their maximum potential and to live their desired life. As CEO of Jessica L Vera PhD LLC, Global Enterprises and Elite Foundation – Elite Performance Academy Equipping Souls for Action, a not-for-profit organization – she collaboratively creates, develops, and distributes cutting-edge informed trainings, assessments, and tools for self and business strategic optimization. Now transitioned from brick and mortar to ecommerce and digital education, her services can be accessed from the comfort of your own computer and through her destination live experiential global events – One Day to Freedom™.

Dr. J. utilizes personal and professional experience, informed evidence-based knowledge and secularized ancient healing practices to heal, equip, and empower others to Change Your Mind. Change Your Life™. Dr. J. is a socially-conscious entrepreneur who has served on numerous prestigious boards and spoken on domestic and international platforms. She is a trauma-graduate, life-learner and heart-led professional who takes full advantage of every opportunity gifted to her, to increase awareness and prevention of human exploitation; and she believes that one of the keys is education. Dr. J. is a passionate activist, who takes her social responsibility to be a voice for victims of social injustice seriously. Dr. J. has been happily married for the last 20 years and has had the privilege of raising two beautiful daughters. Dr. J.'s 21st century legacy goal is to inspire, empower and equip 1,000,000 souls to reach their pinnacle potential for the good of all humanity, through socially-responsible intentional life and business practices by the year 2040.

CHAPTER 23

THE IMPACT OF PRESENCE: THE BIG SECRET TO MEDIA SUCCESS

BY JW DICKS, ESQ. & NICK NANTON, ESQ.

Steven Spielberg is the most famous movie director working today. Starting with Jaws, this prodigy started making movies as a teen with a primitive Super 8 camera. But even at that young age, Spielberg knew that talent wouldn't be enough – not for Hollywood to take him seriously. His father had a connection at Universal Studios and managed to wrangle his 16-year-old boy a limited-time unpaid internship. But when the internship was over, Spielberg found himself shut out from the studio where he was sure his moviemaking dreams would be fulfilled.

So…he changed things up. He knew he didn't have a chance at getting back on the lot in his jeans and t-shirt. So, he started wearing business suits and carrying a briefcase. And with that "costume" in place, he managed to talk his way in past the guard station every day. And he found an office where a female clerical worker would allow him to "camp out" – so he could make calls, work on scripts and network on the lot.

In other words, he assumed the presence of someone who belonged there. And because he knew enough to make that happen, everyone accepted him as though he *did* belong there. At the age of 22, he received his first directing assignment, a television episode starring the legendary actress, Joan Crawford. The studio that hired him?

Universal.

Here's what it comes down to. It doesn't matter how much you know or how much talent you have. If you don't project the proper presence, *you'll never make the impact you're after.* Spielberg knew he had to look and act the part of a studio insider in order to be taken seriously – and that, once he was accepted by the powers-that-be, his talent could take care of the rest.

Well, it turns out there's some very powerful science behind Spielberg's strategy. And in this excerpt from our forthcoming book, *Impact!* we're going to explore the "Big Secret" of how you can make similar tactics work for you.

Probably most of you reading this have gone on a job interview at some point or another. It's one of those situations that totally relies on the kind of impact you're able to make in the room. Think about it – you have to convince someone who's a virtual stranger to hire you, to take you on for forty hours or more a week and entrust an aspect of their business in your hands. Persuading that person can often be a more difficult job than the position you're being considered for.

Well, becoming a MediaMaster—our term for a thought leader who is able to leverage all media opportunities available—is much like preparing for the biggest job interview of your life. However, instead of having to impress one or two executives at a company, you have to impress thousands – or even millions – of people with your persona. You also have a lot less time to make an impression than in a job interview. Studies show you only have anywhere from 8 to 20 seconds to hold the attention of someone watching you in an online video.

That's why *now* – before you even think of appearing in any kind of media – is the time you should be working on *elevating your presence.* You want to be able to showcase the best possible version of yourself in whatever venue you appear, so you can maximize every second of exposure and leverage it to your advantage.

How Presence Can Transform You (Literally)

Is there anyone reading this chapter that hasn't heard of TED talks? If that's the case with you, then run to a computer and watch a few. TED talks in recent years have captured the public's imagination by packing amazing ideas and content into 18 minute on-stage presentations by authorities and personalities from all walks of life. As we write these words, there are over 2400 of these TED talks available – and well over a billion people worldwide have viewed them through their various online distribution channels.

Now, just to be clear, not all TED talks are created equal. Some are vastly more popular than others. And what's interesting is the second most popular TED talk of all time – viewed by over 33 million people around the world – is a TED talk by social psychologist Ann Cuddy on how to use your own body language to appear confident and powerful. In other words, exactly what we're writing about here in this chapter.

Here's an excerpt from that talk – and check out her statistic on political candidates:

"We make sweeping judgments and inferences from body language. And those judgments can predict really meaningful life outcomes like who we hire or promote, who we ask out on a date…Even more dramatic, Alex Todorov at Princeton has shown us that judgments of political candidates' faces in just one second predict 70 percent of U.S. Senate and gubernatorial race outcomes."[1]

Did you read that closely? *One second* can determine whether or not a candidate gets elected. That's how much your first impression might matter to your audience.

So obviously, presence is power. And the massive popularity of Cuddy's topic (so popular that it led to a lucrative book deal for her) indicates that most of us *know* presence means power – and, furthermore, most of us feel we lack it. Frankly, many are afraid they can't pull it off. They focus on their negatives – they're not attractive enough, not smart enough, not rich enough…or maybe they just think their voice sounds funny. But none of these individual factors really matter. Why?

*Because the real secret of creating a powerful presence is being able to tap into your own personal power - a power that **everyone** has.*

1. Transcript of Ann Cuddy TED Talk available online at: https://www.ted.com/talks/amy_cuddy_your_body_language_shapes_who_you_are/transcript?language=en

Oprah, for example, is unquestionably one of the premier MediaMasters of this or any other age. And yet, she grew up wearing potato sacks for clothes in an unbelievably poverty-stricken and abusive childhood. Napoleon Hill, Dale Carnegie and Tony Robbins all came from humble beginnings. None of these people had the kind of formal training most of us assume you need to be successful at using media. However, they instinctively understood the secrets behind creating a memorable impression.

This is precisely Cuddy's point – that anyone can learn these secrets and anyone can easily create a powerful presence, a presence that will, in turn, make *themselves* feel more powerful. And her research proves her point.

Cuddy, along with researchers Dana Carney and Andy Yap, asked male and female participants in their experiment to hold two poses, each for one minute. One pose was a "high power pose" (standing with feet apart while leaning over a table with one hand resting on it or sitting CEO-style with feet on the table and hands behind the head) or a "low power pose" (sitting with shoulders slumped forward and hands in lap - or standing with feet together and arms folded tightly across chest.).

Remember, the men and women were only asked to hold these poses for one minute. And yet, the results were dramatic.

After the high-power poses, the participants reported they felt significantly more powerful and in charge. They were also more willing to take a risk when offered the opportunity to double their earnings from the study by gambling them. And if you think the change was just psychological, think again. The high-power posers also demonstrated big jumps in their testosterone levels as well as neuroendocrine elements that link to competitiveness, dominance and leadership ability. The opposite transformation happened with the low-power posers, who reverted to a nervous, risk-averse mindset (with the corresponding physical changes as well).

To quote from the original study:

In short, posing in displays of power caused advantaged and adaptive psychological, physiological, and behavioral changes, and these findings suggest that embodiment extends beyond mere thinking and feeling, to physiology and subsequent behavioral choices. That a person can, by assuming two simple 1-min poses, embody power and instantly become more powerful has real-world, actionable implications. [2]

To put in simpler terms, that old entrepreneurial motto, "Fake it 'til you make it," has some real wisdom behind it. If you assume a power position, you will project that power – and cause yourself to actually *become* more powerful.

It's all about feeding your brain the right message. If you sit all curled up in a ball or cross your arms across your chest like you're protecting yourself from attack, your mind and body will assume that attitude as real. If, instead, you use expansive body language and carry yourself like the guy in charge, your mind and body will take that to heart.

One thing's for sure – if you do want to create impact, if you are aiming at becoming a MediaMaster, you're going to need presence. And we're going to help you get it.

The Keys to a Powerful Presence

Let's switch gears and share some more revelations from *another* study on presence.

Economist Sylvia Ann Hewlett, the founder and CEO of the Center for Talent Innovation and author of the bestseller *Executive Presence*, put a research team to work and surveyed almost 4000 college-educated professionals to further explore what makes for the most memorable presence. The results boiled it down to three crucial factors:

1) How you look
2) How you communicate
3) How you act [3]

2. Dana R. Carney, Amy J.C. Cuddy, and Andy J. Yap, "Power Posing Brief Nonverbal Displays Affect Neuroendocrine Levels and Risk Tolerance," *Psychological Science,* January 20, 2010
3. Maria Shriver, "Look Like a Leader: Secrets of Executive Presence," NBC News, May 28, 2014, http://www.nbcnews.com/feature/maria-shriver/look-leader-secrets-executive-presence-n116316

Hewlett further broke down the importance of each member of this trio. Surprisingly perhaps, how you look only accounted for 5% of someone's presence. Communication came in at 27% and how you act accounted for a stunning 67%.[4]

And how you act definitely falls into the presentation skills we're talking about. According to Hewlett, "A big part...is a knack for conveying tremendous amounts of knowledge and giving people the impression you could go 'six questions deep' on the subject you're talking about, but in a way that's concise. Attention spans are so short now that, whether it's in a speech or in a meeting, you have to show how you can add value in a way that's both compelling and brief."[5]

What this all comes down to is first mastering your body language to project power and remembering that it isn't just for show. As we already noted, *it actually changes your chemistry and boosts your testosterone level.* Here are more specifics from Cuddy's TED talk:

From their baseline when they come in, high-power people experience about a 20-percent increase, and low-power people experience about a 10-percent decrease (in testosterone) ...two minutes lead to these hormonal changes that configure your brain to basically be either assertive, confident and comfortable, or really stress-reactive, and feeling sort of shut down. And we've all had the feeling, right? So, it seems that our non-verbals do govern how we think and feel about ourselves, so it's not just others, but it's also ourselves...our bodies change our minds.

And again, this is not a cheat – this is actually accessing the tools you possess inside you to make yourself the most powerful representation of you possible.

Authenticity: The Crucial Ingredient to Presence

In the words of Cuddy, "This is not about making up a story and convincing yourself it's true."[6] In other words, as we mentioned earlier, presence is about believing in yourself – as well as believing in your own value and the value of whatever it is you are about to say.

4. Anne Fisher, "Can Presence Be Learned?" Fortune Magazine, June 5, 2014
5. Fisher
6. Martinuzzi

Self-doubt can short circuit that belief and actually cause you to disbelieve in the most important aspects of you and your message. And again, the culprit is that imaginary tiger. If you want to make an impact, you have to thoroughly believe in yourself and your mission, whatever that mission might be. Only your stressful emotions can cause you to disbelieve in those things – and those emotions are what's false.

Maybe you have a naturally powerful presence. If so, that's awesome. But most people don't. If you're someone who needs some help in this area, practice. And keep practicing until you internalize your own personal power. It sounds like a cliché, but, as we hope we've demonstrated, it's all based on very scientific principles. Remember, you're real and the tiger is not – so believe in yourself and not in your fear.

Authenticity is the key here; it's what grounds and amplifies your presence. All the techniques we've discussed in this chapter are meant to empower what you already have inside you. If you don't work on improving your presence, you could be cheating yourself – and underrepresenting your worth and your knowledge. Instead, develop the kind of presence that will cause your intended audience to stand up and take notice of what you have to say.

ACTION STEPS TO BUILDING YOUR PRESENCE

Want to see how you can make everything we've just discussed about presence work for you? In the remainder of this chapter, we're going to share some tips on how to increase your presence through a few simple and practical Action Steps that anyone can do. These Action Steps are paraphrased from Amy Cuddy's new bestseller *Presence*, and will help you boost your presentation skills:[7]

- **Action Step #1: Pay attention to your body.**

  When you head into a stressful situation (such as a webcast or interview), your body responds as if it's in a threatening physical situation. However, a tiger is *not* chasing you (as far as we know – maybe check on breakouts at your local zoo). So, remind yourself that your body is overreacting and adjust your posture so it's expansive, not closed up.

7. Bruna Martinuzzi, "Amy Cuddy, Body Language Expert, Reveals What It Takes to Have 'Presence," American Express Open Forum, https://www.americanexpress.com/us/small-business/openforum/articles/amy-cuddy-body-language-presence/

- **Action Step #2: Take two minutes before a presentation to increase your presence.**

  Cuddy advises that you take a couple of minutes before doing a presentation or appearing on camera to work on your body posture and increase the power of your presence. This is enough time to create the needed chemical changes that will boost your confidence and cause you to appear in control and authoritative.

- **Action Step #3: Continue to keep tabs on your stance.**

  If you stop monitoring your posture, your body language can easily collapse. Your shoulders can slump or you might close up your arms in a defensive move. Be aware of when this happens and adjust – after a while, this kind of adjustment will become a habit without you even having to be conscious of it.

- **Action Step #4: Keep track of triggers.**

  If you do find your body language making a negative change, try to identify what caused the change. Even ask yourself what things in your life make you feel powerless. When you understand your problem areas, you can gain more control of your mind-body connection.

- **Action Step #5: Master your body language adjustments.**

  To transform your body language and increase your presence, force your shoulders open and don't allow your chest to go concave. Stretch yourself out – move around if you have to – and even rest your hands on a table or podium to make sure your body is staying open.

- **Action Step #6: Watch your breathing.**

  Breathing is also affected when our mentality becomes one of fight-or-flight. But again, let's remember – there is NO tiger! So, pause and deliberately slow your breathing, as it will speed up when your nervous system feels threatened. By slowing your breathing, you signal your system that you are in rest-and-digest mode – which makes you feel safe.

- **Action Step #7: Slow your speech.**

When you're nervous, you also tend to speak faster. And that also feeds into a bad mind-body message, because fast speech makes you feel less powerful and appear less powerful. Have faith that your message is going to be one that an audience wants to hear – and demonstrate confidence when you speak. *(Mea Culpa: Nick regularly violates this rule!)*

- **Action Step #8: Be confident, not cocky**

Don't misunderstand what's being said here; being confident does not mean being arrogant or defensive. When people are truly self-assured and displaying positive presence, they feel relaxed enough to let their guard down – and are able to hear criticism without responding in an angry or hurtful manner. This is often what you recognize as "authenticity" in others. You don't have to act like you have all the answers, because nobody does.

- **Action Step #9: Set an alert**

Finally, use today's sophisticated smartphones to your advantage. At the beginning of your process to develop presence, set an alert on your phone that will remind you to check your body language and make sure you're keeping it on track. If you find it's not where you want it, quickly correct it. By doing this, you'll develop an instinctive awareness of when your posture is changing, so you can quickly change your stance.

Practice these basics of presence and you'll soon discover your presentation skills markedly improving. It's an amazing way to pump up your impact and leave your audience hungry for more!

About JW

JW Dicks, Esq., is a Wall Street Journal Best-Selling Author®, Emmy Award-Winning Producer, publisher, board member, and co-founder of organizations such as The National Academy of Best-Selling Authors®, and The National Association of Experts, Writers and Speakers®.

JW is the CEO of DNAgency and is a strategic business development consultant to both domestic and international clients. He has been quoted on business and financial topics in national media such as *USA Today, The Wall Street Journal, Newsweek, Forbes, CNBC.com,* and *Fortune Magazine Small Business.*

Considered a thought leader and curator of information, JW has more than forty-three published business and legal books to his credit and has co-authored with legends like Jack Canfield, Brian Tracy, Tom Hopkins, Dr. Nido Qubein, Dr. Ivan Misner, Dan Kennedy, and Mari Smith. He is the Editor and Publisher of *ThoughtLeader® Magazine.*

JW is called the "Expert to the Experts" and has appeared on business television shows airing on ABC, NBC, CBS, and FOX affiliates around the country and co-produces and syndicates a line of franchised business television show such as *Success Today, Wall Street Today, Hollywood Live*, and *Profiles of Success.* He has received an Emmy® Award as Executive Producer of the film, *Mi Casa Hogar.*

JW and his wife of forty-three years, Linda, have two daughters, three granddaughters, and two Yorkies. He is a sixth-generation Floridian and splits his time between his home in Orlando and his beach house on Florida's west coast.

About Nick

An Emmy Award-Winning Director and Producer, Nick Nanton, Esq., produces media and branded content for top thought leaders and media personalities around the world. Recognized as a leading expert on branding and storytelling, Nick has authored more than two dozen Best-Selling books (including the Wall Street Journal Best-Seller, *StorySelling™)* and produced and directed more than 40 documentaries, earning 5 Emmy Awards and 14 nominations. Nick speaks to audiences internationally on the topics of branding, entertainment, media, business and storytelling at major universities and events.

As the CEO of DNA Media, Nick oversees a portfolio of companies including: The Dicks + Nanton Agency (an international agency with more than 3000 clients in 36 countries), Dicks + Nanton Productions, Ambitious.com, CelebrityPress, DNA Films®, DNA Pulse, and DNA Capital Ventures. Nick is an award-winning director, producer and songwriter who has worked on everything from large-scale events to television shows with the likes of Steve Forbes, Ivanka Trump, Sir Richard Branson, Rudy Ruettiger (inspiration for the Hollywood blockbuster, "Rudy"), Jack Canfield (*The Secret*, creator of the *Chicken Soup for the Soul* Series), Brian Tracy, Michael E. Gerber, Tom Hopkins, Dan Kennedy and many more.

Nick has been seen in *USA Today, The Wall Street Journal, Newsweek, BusinessWeek, Inc. Magazine, The New York Times, Entrepreneur® Magazine, Forbes,* and *FastCompany.* He has appeared on ABC, NBC, CBS, and FOX television affiliates across the country as well as on CNN, FOX News, CNBC, and MSNBC from coast to coast.

Nick is a member of the Florida Bar, a voting member of The National Academy of Recording Arts & Sciences (Home to The GRAMMYs), a member of The National Academy of Television Arts & Sciences (Home to the EMMYs), Co-founder of The National Academy of Best-Selling Authors®, and serves on the Innovation Board of the XPRIZE Foundation, a non-profit organization dedicated to bringing about "radical breakthroughs for the benefit of humanity" through incentivized competition – best known for it's Ansari XPRIZE which incentivized the first private space flight and was the catalyst for Richard Branson's Virgin Galactic. Nick also enjoys serving as an Elder at Orangewood Church, working with Young Life, Downtown Credo Orlando, Entrepreneurs International and rooting for the Florida Gators with his wife Kristina and their three children, Brock, Bowen and Addison.

Learn more at:
- www.NickNanton.com
- www.CelebrityBrandingAgency.com